Creating

Home

Sanctuaries

with Feng Shui

Sacred Spaces, Altars, and Shrines

SHAWNE MITCHELL
WITH STEPHANIE GUNNING

NEW PAGE BOOKS
A division of The Career Press, Inc.
Franklin Lakes, NJ

CREATING HOME SANCTUARIES WITH FENG SHUI
EDITED BY KATE PRESTON
TYPESET BY STACEY A. FARKAS
ILLUSTRATIONS BY JANICE BLAIR
Cover design by Lu Rossman/Digi Dog Design
Printed in the U.S.A. by Book-mart Press

To order this title, please call toll-free 1-800-CAREER-1 (NJ and Canada: 201-848-0310) to order using VISA or MasterCard, or for further information on books from Career Press.

The Career Press, Inc., 3 Tice Road, PO Box 687,
Franklin Lakes, NJ 07417
www.careerpress.com
www.newpagebooks.com

Library of Congress Cataloging-in-Publication Data
Mitchell, Shawne, 1958-
    Creating home sanctuaries with feng shui : sacred spaces, altars, and shrines / by Shawne Mitchell with Stephanie Gunning.
        p. cm.
    Includes bibliographical references and index.
    ISBN 1-56414-570-0 (pbk.)
    1. Feng shui. I. Gunning, Stephanie, 1962- II. Title.

BF1779.F4 M57 2003
133.3'337—dc21   2002026409

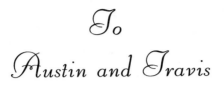

To
Austin and Travis

Acknowledgments

I 'm delighted to lovingly thank Stephanie Gunning, a true "patron saint" for writers. Her wisdom, patience, inspiration, and exemplary writing skills have contributed much to this book. And her collaboration made this project fun. I thank her with all my heart!

I am blessed and honored to love, and be loved, by my sons, Austin and Travis Cook. I treasure them both beyond words and thank them for their patience, humor, and youthful wisdom and insight!

Special thanks to my agent, Stephany Evans for making everything happen. She has been such a wonderful support.

Sincere gratitude and appreciation to Janice Blair for her beautiful illustrations.

Also, to the editors at New Page Books, Mike Lewis and Kate Preston: Thank you so much.

I am also grateful for the support, friendship, and wisdom of all those who have helped me both directly and indirectly on my life path to share the loving energy of Spirit including Arielle, Deborah, Juliet, Denise, Satsuki, Jo Ann, Cherie, and J.D.

Heartfelt love and deep thanks to my parents in heaven, Nona and King, and to my brothers, Richard, Chris, Mitch, Ryan, and Dan, and their families for providing a foundation of love and support. I know I am very blessed.

Lastly, thank you God for allowing me to share a lifestyle aligned with the soul—my Soul Style.

Contents

Your Home as a Sacred Sanctuary

"To be happy at home is the ultimate result of all ambition."
—*Samuel Johnson*

Throughout history, people have sought to commune with the Divine and bring sacred energy into the everyday world. Ancient farmers made offerings to the gods to reap a bountiful harvest from the fields. Fisher folk asked for blessings on their ships to increase the yield of the catch and feed their children. Healer-priests prayed in temples for spiritual intervention for those they served. And artists honored the muses of inspiration in marble, on canvas, or on a paper. What the field, ship, temple, and artist media have always had in common is that they were vessels for the Divine on Earth. People knew that libations, burnt offerings, and other forms of worship would bring abundance, creativity, health, and community if sacred energy filled their lives.

A contemporary home is no less a vessel for the sacred than a temple is, although we may not believe it possible because "ordinary life" goes on within. Over time, many of us came to believe the notion that God lives separately inside churches, synagogues, and temples. Because these buildings are often exquisite and uplifting, sometimes designed with high, vaulted ceilings, stained glass windows, and gleaming golden artifacts, it is easy to forget that they are not the only focal points available to celebrate the essence of the Divine. A home can also overflow with sanctity if we pay it respectful attention. In fact, the home is almost *always* a mirror that reflects what we cherish and find valuable: our most beloved others, our selves, the mementos of our lives, and our highest aspirations. Why shouldn't we celebrate the Divine and enjoy its sacred blessings in our everyday spaces?

Years ago, I attended a lecture given by Thomas Moore, author of *Care of the Soul*. He spoke about his hobby of handcrafting wooden furniture for his home (tables, chairs, shelves, and cabinets). He described how, as he lovingly and patiently carved, sawed, and planed, the pieces became imbued with his soul essence. The moment he said this, it was as though a lightning bolt had shot straight through my body, jolting my mind, my heart, and my soul. *Of course!* I thought gleefully. *Your soul imprints your belongings with its energy.* I had already been in real estate for 15 years and it seemed obvious in and relevant to my past experiences.

Even though I knew nothing about the art of feng shui, as a Realtor I had always been able to sense the subtle energy in a house. Like a tuning fork, I would respond to the emotional undercurrents in the places I went, knowing intuitively whether the inhabitants were happy, sad, loving, or angry. During my career, I'd literally visited thousands of properties, and understood that I was affected by intangible, as well as aesthetic, considerations. Similarly, people coming to my own house often said, "Wow! Your home *feels* so good." I began mulling it over: *What is it about a home that makes it feel a certain way?*

So, hearing Moore's comments, I found the answer: *The people who live there endow their home with an energetic signature.* My insight was the permission I needed to begin advising my clients about specific ways to find and create homes that would both please their senses and nourish their souls. And they loved it! My business expanded in new directions.

Before long, I was studying the Black Hat Sect School of feng shui, which is based on Tibetan Tantric Buddhism. I also traveled around the world and conducted my own research on the historical significance of sacred spaces, shrines, and altars. Having been raised a Catholic, I had always been a spiritual seeker. I incorporated what I had learned of Hinduism and Zen Buddhism, along with my experiences as a student of Transcendental Meditation and of the teachings of Parmahansa Yogananda, into my burgeoning perspective on home design. It was intriguing that the discoveries by quantum physicists about energy echoed the beliefs of ancient mystics about Spirit. Gradually, I developed a vocabulary with which to communicate the ideas that you'll find in the pages of this book.

But, before you dive in, it's important to be clear about a few concepts.

Sanctuaries, Altars, and Shrines

Traditionally, sanctuaries are the holiest spaces within a temple. In a Christian church, for instance, the sanctuary is the area that holds the altar. In a Jewish synagogue, it's where they keep the Ark. Looking even further back, all ancient Egyptian temples had an interior room, the "Holiest of Holies," which was the exclusive provenance of priests or priestesses. In every age and religion, these areas have been considered sacrosanct and revered. Sanctuaries are also places of refuge from danger and for retreat from the impurities of the world.

Every room in your home can be a sanctuary for your soul. Your home is an intimate retreat from the world, a place to let down your guard, slow your pace, and relax in the company of loved ones. It is a place to express your creativity, be spontaneous, and indulge your senses. You can also be highly emotional in the privacy of your home, or quiet, without worrying about disrupting others or having to cater to their needs. Furthermore, a home is a crucible to strengthen the bonds of marriage and family.

Altars originally were places to make ritual sacrifices and special offerings to appease the tribal gods or ask them for favors, such as a successful hunt, abundant crops, or victory in battle. Early cultures usually built their altars in the hills or mountains, so the word altar translates, in Latin, to "high," meaning close to heaven. Altars have always been used to attract the purest and most revered forces, like a lightning rod. To the present day, altars are power spots where people do rituals and other kinds of spiritual work.

Shrines are slightly different than altars. They are devotional sites that began as niches or crevasses in rock outcroppings and were used to hold sacred objects. Inside Catholic churches you can find many shrines that honor individual saints and angels. Here, visitors and pilgrims requesting an intercession for a loved one have lit candles, set down photographs, and tucked notes, flowers, and other tokens. You may also have noticed makeshift shrines along roads or highways where people's friends or loved ones have lost their lives. Do you recall the memorial shrine of flowers that blossomed in front of Kensington Palace after Lady Diana's tragic death?

In modern homes, you can find spiritual shrines dedicated to admired religious figures and deities, along with many non-spiritual shrines dedicated to pursuits we love, such as collections of baseball cards, decorative plates, and theatrical memorabilia. Our souls are comforted and nourished by the meaning of these belongings, as Thomas Moore's soul flourished in the presence of the furniture he lovingly created.

Feng Shui, Energy, and Sacred Space

Through the application and influence of certain feng shui principles, you can build home sanctuaries that will attract positive spiritual energy into your home. **Feng shui** (pronounced *fung shway*) is the study of life force energy, or chi (pronounced *chee*), and how it moves around us and through our environments. Everything in the universe is made up of this same fundamental energy, which ebbs, flows, and intersects in different patterns. Chi is alive, it has intelligence, and no matter what form it takes—whether a meadow, a river, an animal, a building, soap bubbles, or a sacred altar—it is always in relationship to everything else and, thus, can be influenced. Feng shui practitioners hold this vision of connection in mind so we can purposefully direct, regulate, and enhance the flow of positive energy in our surroundings.

The art of feng shui originated more than 4,000 years ago in China, created by tribal healers and spiritual leaders who took responsibility for the health and prosperity of the people. This entailed choosing locations for villages and farms in landscapes sheltered from the wind and near water. The phrase feng shui literally translates as "wind water." Over centuries of persistent observation of nature, they understood what was beneficial and set down principles. Different schools of thought developed. The *Form School* focused on the shape of the terrain. The *Compass School* invented a grid that divided the environment into sectors corresponding to the directions and also to an ancient system of mystical divination called the I Ching (also known as *The Book of Changes*). These and other specific principles have been passed down to modern practitioners.

In the United States, the predominant school of classical feng shui is the Black Hat Sect. Based in part on Tibetan Buddhism, like the Compass School, it maps the environment—a property, floor plan, or single room—but orients the map according to the location of the main entrance, the "mouth of chi," rather than the cardinal directions. Lately, practitioners have also been evolving an even less traditional approach, which for the purposes of this book I call **Intuitive Feng Shui**. This is extremely attractive to Westerners because it empowers us to draw upon the materials of many religious and secular traditions from a vast cross section of cultures.

In the United States, as a result of being a cultural and ethnic melting pot, you can find a smorgasbord of types of altars, shrines, and sacred spaces in homes. Many of our immigrants have strongly influenced the popular imagination with their rituals and artifacts. It is quite common nowadays to see a Hindu figurine of the elephant-headed god Ganesh side by side on a tabletop with a Jewish menorah or a statue of the Virgin Mary. You can hardly visit a garden nursery anywhere in the country without noticing Quan Yin, the Chinese goddess of compassion, radiating benevolence among the greens.

In this book, if I succeed in conveying nothing else, I want you to understand that you must resonate *from the heart* with the furnishings in your home. The soul loves the experience of sacred energy; it finds it pleasing and harmonious. That's how you know you're in a place of communion with the Divine. Remarkably, what gives us that experience is unique for each individual. For some, it's mystical artifacts from temples; for others, it's the blossom of a flower or the smile of a child.

How to Use This Book

There's been a tremendous amount of mystery surrounding the principles of feng shui in the past. However, I think it is important to acknowledge that it is also a very intuitive art. This being the case, we must learn to listen to the subtle and not-so-subtle messages of our intuition and our souls. So, along with reading this book, it's a good idea to practice meditation or contemplation on a regular basis. Then, read one chapter at a time and put the suggestions to work. Let the ideas sink in, look around your home, evaluate, do the activities, and *live* with the transformation before moving on.

Right away, you should sense a shift in the subtle energy. Nonetheless, it is always important to note that something *seemingly* negative might first occur when you make a feng shui adjustment in your environment. Be patient, sometimes that's what is necessary in order to remove an obstacle or blockage. Afterwards, the positive energy can flow more effortlessly.

The first chapter is going to help you get a sense of the spirit of your home as it is right now, and your home is going to tell you how it feels. During dialogues with different rooms, you may be astonished to find out what's been lurking beneath your conscious awareness. Now your needs and the needs of your home will become self-evident.

Chapter 2 deals with decluttering and purification. This is a tremendously important step because you have to get rid of the old to bring in the new. You will ultimately be activating the energy of your surroundings and you don't want to reawaken stale, old, "funky" energy. There is some magic in space clearing. It's not something that a scientist would be able to explain. And blowing smoke around a house or banging a drum might seem "airy" to a skeptic. But once you try it, you'll notice that it works.

After space clearing you will be selecting energy enhancements (in Chapter 3) that will positively charge the energy field in your home so it supports your new intentions. In feng shui, these would be called "cures," but the ones I describe aren't only Chinese; they include Native American medicine wheels and labyrinths, for example. Energy enhancements include colors, smells, and sounds.

When you're gathering ingredients and power tools, as suggested in Chapter 4, let your imagination roam freely. This section contains a whole host of possibilities, but it really can only scratch the surface. Use it to stimulate your thought processes and figure out what might appeal best to your individual soul.

In Chapters 5 through 8 we'll explore communal, intimate, creative, and contemplative areas of your home and garden. You may skip around and go directly to the topic that interests you most. However, reading all of the chapters will contribute ideas to any room or type of area, as there's an overlap. For instance, a bathroom can be communal (think of bathing your children) as well as intimate (think of taking a relaxing bath alone). Similarly, a dining room is communal (think dinner party), but it can also be a zone of creativity (think of spreading out a project on the table).

In the final chapter, Sacred Rituals, you'll learn how to activate the energy of your altars, shrines, and sacred spaces with ceremonies. These include rituals for life transitions, such as marriage and divorce, graduation, and the birth of a baby; holidays; changes of the seasons; and daily prayers and meditations.

In essence, this book will teach you a seven-stage process for setting and manifesting your spiritual intentions.

The Alchemy of Intention

Where intention goes, energy flows. Because of how energy functions, we are each engaged in co-creation with the life force. If you want your life to be sacred, you need to set the intention for it to be so. Setting an intention is like speaking to the Divine through a megaphone: it gets the message across more clearly. This is the true secret behind creating a home sanctuary. Altars and shrines are incredible spiritual tools because they anchor our feelings and thoughts so we become very clear and specific about what we want. Ultimately, whatever we focus on appears in the material world.

Creating a sacred space in your home is an opportunity to connect your intimate environment with the realm of the Divine so that your soul is supported and nourished and has freedom to express and flourish.

Chapter 1

Identifying Your Sacred Space

"The real voyage of discovery consists not in seeking new landscapes, but in having new eyes."
—*Marcel Proust*

*E*veryone has a personal vision of a sacred space. Your vision could be a quiet spot to practice yoga, create art, or write in your journal. Perhaps you want to find the best place for meditation, prayer, or to create an altar or shrine. In this chapter, you'll learn to conduct the search for an ideal location in which to honor that vision by using the feng shui mapping device known as the **bagua** and two intuitive activities. In order to learn about your home and align it to your soul, it is important to connect with the divinity of its different areas. For, just as every person's individual essence is different, so is the essence of every room in your home and every area of your garden.

I suggest you begin planning your sacred space by giving some thought to the purpose it will serve. Remember: Everything in our lives comes into being from the initial impetus of our thoughts. By contemplating how you will use your sacred space, you can begin to put your specific intentions into motion. This same process will also help you later when it comes time to choose energy enhancements and ingredients to furnish it.

Finding Your Sacred Space

Several considerations can contribute to finding your sacred space. Sometimes placement and orientation are influenced by personal preference, and other times by such factors as the bagua, an eight-sided diagram that overlays the environment you are working upon. These days, our living spaces are typically smaller, so many of us must "search out" a sacred space even when it imposes on other spaces in a home. You must consider the size of the available locations in your home or on your property.

The following activity may facilitate the process of identifying a sacred space.

TAKE A SPIRITUAL JOURNEY

Before you begin, sit down, close your eyes, and spend a few minutes in silence. The point is to quiet your mind and experience increased clarity and intuition. When you feel relaxed and centered, open your eyes and stand up. You'll now take a spiritual walk around your home. Start at your front gate, or the place where your property emerges distinctly from your neighbor's.

A cozy garden sanctuary

Look around your garden, patio, terrace, balcony, deck, or porch. Is there a wonderful shady tree in your yard? Do you have an old tool- or gardening-shed, greenhouse, barn, or outbuilding that you could salvage, clean up, and transform?

Following the path to your front door, notice how you feel. Take your time. Look around and observe anything that makes your emotions and subtle energy rise or fall. For instance, do you have a pot of flowers at your front door? Are they blooming or wilting? How does it make you feel if they are wilting? Do you have a gate latch that is broken or in need of some repair? Notice whether you feel disturbed about anything that's broken or in disrepair. Are your front windows clean? Is the shrubbery pruned and tidy?

As you stand before your front door, observe: Is your door clean? Is your doormat in good condition? Is the hardware attractive? If you've hung a wreath, are its greens and flowers fresh, or old and wilted? Does the doorbell have a pleasant chime? Notice how this area feels and what kind of responses it provokes in you.

Then, open your front door and enter your home. Be "present" to what is around you. Walk from room to room. Look for any space that could be transformed into an altar or sanctuary. Keep in mind your sacred purpose.

Start in your living room: Is there a table, window seat, shelf, or cabinet that you could use? Is the room designed in an L-shape, so you could screen off a separate area?

Do you have a den or home office that contains similar areas?

In your kitchen: Do you have a breakfast corner that could be transformed into a sacred space? A cozy nook can go from feeding your body to feeding your soul!

In the bedroom: Screen-off a corner for an altar or shrine. Look again for a cabinet, shelf, window seat, or niche.

Do you have a spare bedroom? If so, consider yourself blessed. It is as if the universe has handed you your sanctuary on a silver platter! A guestroom that is rarely occupied can double as a home sanctuary for you or pampered guests.

A spacious bathroom can be a relaxing and healing sanctuary or spa. Devote a corner of it to an altar. Perhaps you own a small cabinet or linen closet whose door you could remove. Then you might arrange a small altar or shrine on its shelves.

Is there spare space in the basement or attic? You'll never know until you really start hunting and noticing what's hidden in these unexplored and untended areas.

Rest assured, the "right" place will speak to you. You will intuitively recognize it. The intentions you made earlier will direct you and "bring into existence" the space that is appropriate. Forget any preconceived ideas of what a sacred space "should" be.

After you have made your journey, review your list of potential areas, using these questions: Which place seems the most practical? Did one area in particular resonate with you? Did you want a place that was private? Do you need to confer with other family members? Are they participating in this sojourn with you? How will they be impacted? Taking all these things into consideration is going to make your final selection process much easier.

Shifting From Hectic to Serene

Jaclyn is a busy woman. When I met her, she was a graduate student writing her master's thesis, wife to a successful executive, and mom to two children ages 11 and 14. To combat the stress of her hectic schedule, Jaclyn had been learning how to meditate. Unfortunately, carving out time to write her thesis was hard enough, let alone finding time and privacy to meditate. She knew she needed a quiet, spiritual place to call her own. That's when she called me for a consultation.

Jaclyn did a mindfulness walk around her entire property (including her garden) and every part of the house (including the garage) allowing her inner voice to lead her. She discovered that the room that resonated most for her was the little office where she wrote. Jaclyn, her husband, and the kids discussed it, and they all agreed that she would "take over" the home office as her personal domain.

To create a simple meditation zone in her office, she transformed a cabinet holding books and research material into an altar. On the shelves and cubbies that had once held books, she placed figurines depicting different deities, such as Quan Yin, Jesus, Buddha, and a fertility goddess, along with photos, candles, incense holders, crystals,

Jaclyn's cabinet altar

gemstones, her favorite meditation books, a vase of flowers, and some personal mementos. She placed a couple of old prayer rugs on the floor that she had found in the flea markets of Marrakech when she was a young traveler. Then she bought yoga pads and meditation cushions and placed these on the rugs in front of the cabinet. Jaclyn began adding appropriate energy enhancements and ingredients a few at a time to allow her to carefully handcraft the energy of her altar and meditation space. Now, twice a day, in the morning and evening, Jaclyn meditates in her personal sacred space.

The Bagua Map

The bagua is a template, or grid, developed by feng shui practitioners long ago in order to map the environment. It is borrowed from the I Ching, also known as *The Book of Changes*, which is an ancient Chinese divination system and guide to right action. The eight quadrants, or zones, of the bagua correspond with and also govern specific aspects of our life experience. They are known as:

- Journey and Career.
- Self-Wisdom and Knowledge.
- Family and Health.
- Prosperity and Abundance.
- Fame and Reputation.
- Marriage and Relationship.
- Children and Creativity.
- Helpful Friends and Travel.

Prosperity and Abundance	Fame and Reputation	Marriage and Relationships
Family and Health		Children and Creativity
Self-Wisdom and Knowledge	Journey and Career	Helpful Friends and Travel

The feng shui bagua

When you overlay the bagua on your land, home, room, or even altar, it is possible to identify where these different zones are located. Study each one and then, if necessary, improve and enhance the life force, or flow of chi in that area. Boosting the energy of a zone in your home sanctuary or on your altar will magnify the benefits you desire in the part of your life that is represented by the bagua zone. For instance, if you intend to increase your income, you can locate a prosperity altar in the bagua zone of Prosperity and Abundance in your home office. You could create an altar in this same zone in every other room of your house and your garden, too, for good measure.

The easiest way to begin using the bagua template is to draw a floor plan of the area you want to work on. If you want to enhance the sacred energy of your entire home, then begin with the floor plan of your home. If you have already identified a certain room or an area of your garden as the location for your sacred space, altar, or shrine, then draw an outline of that particular room or garden area.

Don't worry about being 100 percent accurate. Just draw the general idea of the layout of the space. Graph paper can be helpful with this exercise.

Now, trace the illustration of the bagua template onto tracing paper. You may want to make several copies, or to get it enlarged at the copy shop. The tracing paper allows you to overlay the bagua map on your floor plan or garden plan to identify the placement of the various life zones.

To align your bagua template accurately, you'll need to locate what feng shui calls the **mouth of chi**. This is the main entrance, opening, or doorway into your home, room, or garden, which is where energy first enters your space—often powerfully. If you were creating an altar or shrine on a tabletop, then the mouth of chi would be in the front middle section of the table.

By the way, not all schools of feng shui have the same idea about the orientation of the bagua, and some even hold contradictory views. For our purposes, we are going to use the Black Hat School method.

Once you've found the mouth of chi, align the front entrance or door with one of the following bagua zones, starting from the left-hand side of the map: Self-Wisdom and Knowledge, Journey and Career, or Helpful Friends and Travel. This is determined purely by whether the entrance is situated on the left-hand side of the building or room, in the middle, or on the right-hand side of the building or room as you face into it.

This system remains the same whether you are aligning the bagua to the front of your plot of land, house, or apartment; an individual doorway to a room or the entrance to your garden; or your desktop or a tabletop where you are about to build an altar.

Do you begin to see how the different parts of your home or rooms align with the different zones of the bagua? Now you can play with, and explore the unique influences of each bagua zone in your life. Here are some basic guidelines.

Journey and Career

The zone of Journey and Career is located in the bottom center of the bagua. The color associated with it, and that can enhance its energy, is *black*. The element that is associated with this zone is *Water*, which symbolizes the flow of life—your journey.

Your life's journey is in balance when you are aligned with a purpose. You have both an outer purpose and an inner purpose. Your outer purpose is to make a contribution through work. This contribution is not an end in itself; it is a pathway that leads you through your life. It suggests that you consciously and decidedly forge your *own* path, not one trail-blazed by another. You also have an inner purpose. This is a journey of self-discovery. It is the path to your soul, or inner divinity.

Enhance the energy of the zone of Journey and Career when:

- You plan to redirect your life's purpose.
- You want to reinvent yourself.
- You are seeking to change careers.
- You want to discover your life's purpose.

To amplify the energy of this zone, look through the power tools and ingredients in Chapter 4 to find items that incorporate water. For instance, you could install a fountain or an aquarium. Consider a chandelier if the entrance to your home is in this zone. Place a cut glass prism in this zone on an altar table. Place art here that depicts oceans, lakes, or rivers. If the zone aligns with your front door, you might lacquer your front door black.

You can infuse and increase the chi of this area with symbols of your life purpose or career. If your path is a spiritual one, you may want to place a statue of the Buddha near your front door. If your career is in the teaching professions, you might place books about your favorite topics here.

Self-Wisdom and Knowledge

This zone of the bagua is located in the lower left-hand corner. The color that is associated with it, and that enhances its energy, is *blue*. *Mountains* rule this zone. It generates their magnificence and stillness; supports self-awareness, meditation, prayer; and practices and disciplines contributing to self-growth. These include both spiritual activities, such as yoga or tai chi, and scholarly learning, such as taking classes and going to lectures.

A harmonious life is achieved through cultivating a balance between the inner world and the outer world. In our modern hectic times it is very important to sustain inner well-being through a regular practice of meditation, prayer, or yoga. In addition, we need to continue to study the world at large and learn more about ourselves.

Enhance this area of your sacred space when:

- ◆ You are practicing spiritual exercises, such as yoga.
- ◆ You want to create a sanctuary for meditation or prayer.
- ◆ You are studying, learning, or reading.
- ◆ You want to foster your connection with the Divine.

This is a particularly good zone of the home to locate a meditation sanctuary, a den for study, or a shrine or an altar. To heighten the chi of this zone, you can hang pictures of mountains in it, paint the walls blue, arrange figurines of your spiritual teachers on an altar, or start a library in it of books on self-growth or other subjects.

Family and Health

The zone of Family and Health is located in the center left-hand side of the bagua. The color associated with it, and that can enhance its energy, is *green*, and the element is *Wood*. It is governed by *thunder*. Feng shui tradition teaches that thunder is symbolic of the voice of your ancestors and teachers. When your ancestors are happy, it is believed to result in health and good fortune.

This zone also represents your familial relationships and close friendships. Good friends and a stable family are the foundations of well-being. When your emotional and physical health has been secured, you will experience blessings and good fortune.

Enhance this zone of your sacred space when:

- ◆ You are (or a loved one is) experiencing a health challenge.
- ◆ You want to heal a family crisis.

* You are dieting or on a fitness program.
* You need support from family or friends.

This is a good zone for a shrine devoted to family. For instance, if you have a table located in this zone, you could place a collection of framed photographs of your family members atop it. This is also the best zone in which to locate an altar for someone who is planning to have surgery or has a serious illness. Create an altar using green candles, flowers, and photos of that person in good health, as well as other healing symbols.

Prosperity and Abundance

The zone of Prosperity and Abundance is located in the upper left-hand corner of the bagua. This zone is ruled by *Wind*, which, like the element of *Water*, symbolizes the flow of good fortune and wealth. The color that enhances its energy is *purple*.

Although many people associate abundance solely with money, in actuality it pertains to everything of value—health and relationships, as much as material goods. This zone governs the steady accumulation of wealth and other resources in order to provide you with stability and security.

Enhance this zone of your sacred space when:

* You want to increase your income.
* You are struggling financially.
* You would like to feel more secure.
* You are embarking on a new business venture.

In your home, this is a good zone for an office. On your desktop, you can enhance this area with objects that signify money and prosperity, purple accessories, or a vase of purple flowers. Water features, such as an indoor fountain or an aquarium, would also amplify the energy of this zone.

Fame and Reputation

The bagua zone of Fame and Reputation is located in the top center of the map. The color that enhances its energy is *red*, and the feng shui element for this area is *Fire*. Fire signifies your inner light, integrity, and trust. These are the qualities of a person with a good reputation.

This zone correlates with your contributions to your community—both your business community and your social community. A good reputation helps attract opportunity and good fortune. The Fame and Reputation zone also represents your self-esteem and level of confidence.

Enhance this zone of your sacred space when:

- ◆ You would like to increase your sphere of influence.
- ◆ You want more recognition in your business and community.
- ◆ You lack confidence.
- ◆ You need to repair your reputation.

From a spiritual perspective, this is a good zone to energize when you want to deepen your spiritual path, as it represents illumination. Elements and attributes that stimulate its energy include red objects, such as red flowers or candles, and symbols of enlightenment, such as religious figurines or mystical artifacts. Use these ingredients on an altar in this area of your sanctuary. To foster recognition, display awards or other symbols of your accomplishments.

Marriage and Relationship

The zone of Marriage and Relationship is located in the upper right-hand corner of the bagua. The color that enhances this zone is *pink*, and it is associated with the element of *Earth*. Earth energy represents the sacred feminine, or receptive, principle of unconditional love.

On a physical level, this zone governs love relationships of a traditional and non-traditional nature. It represents partnerships of all kinds. On a spiritual level, it embodies your love for yourself. It is through loving and accepting ourselves that we develop the capacity to love another.

Enhance this bagua zone when:

- ◆ You want to attract love.
- ◆ You have made poor love choices.

- You are forming a new business partnership.
- You want to emotionally heal and nurture yourself.

This is a good place to locate an altar for romance. Use objects with qualities related to the Earth, such as pottery and earthenware. Think in terms of pairs, such as a pair of candlesticks or a sculpture of a couple in an embrace. Use the color pink: pink candles, pink roses, and pink hearts. Hang pictures of lovers and affirmations of love on the walls.

Children and Creativity

The Children and Creativity zone of the bagua is located in the center right-hand side. The color that enhances this area is *white*, and it is ruled by the element of *Metal*. Its feng shui symbol is the *lake*, representing deep stillness, or a well of new life. Thus it is related to fertility, children, and creativity. When heightened, this zone fosters and inspires the creative spirit and the inner child, as well as benefiting all the children in the household.

Enhance this area of your sacred space when:

- You are trying to have a baby.
- You have children in your home.
- You want to attract creative inspiration.
- You are a professional artist (or an aspiring one).

A sacred altar in this zone would support becoming pregnant. For an uninspired writer or fine artist, this would be a good place for an altar to foster creation. Use artifacts from your field of endeavor, such as sheet music, instruments, inspiring quotations, esteemed books, paintbrushes, or whatever honors the spirit of your particular art form. Place metal objects here, such as silver candlesticks or a bronze sculpture.

Helpful Friends and Travel

This zone is located in the lower right-hand corner of the bagua. The color associated with it, and that enhances its energy is *gray*. In feng shui, it is associated with the symbol for *heaven*. In other words, helpful friends can be earthly or otherworldly, such as saints and angels. When you enhance this area, you are calling upon Divine Benefactors.

This zone also is symbolic of travel. So if you want to take more trips, enhance the energy here. Who knows? You might unexpectedly win a vacation getaway!

Enhance this sacred zone when:

- ✦ You are looking for investors.
- ✦ You want to connect with spiritual teachers and guides.
- ✦ You would like to travel more frequently.
- ✦ You are praying for a safe trip.

This zone is perfect for a meditation sanctuary because it is associated with the heavenly realms. It is also a good place to arrange images or figurines of spiritual masters and favorite deities. They are a symbolic reminder of the intersection of humanity and divinity. Create an altar here representing sacred sites, diverse cultures, and adventure.

◆ ◆ ◆

As a practical tool, you can use the bagua to decide where to place specific furnishings and objects. When it is applied to any room in your home, it can shift the energy and make it a sacred space that contributes to the abundance, prosperity, love, joy, and well-being in your home and life. This system, coupled with the intuitive wisdom of your soul, can assist you in creating a favorable flow of chi.

If there is a certain aspect of your life that you feel is out of balance, or a part of life that you want to enhance, the bagua is a valuable tool to identify the areas in your environment that "govern" it. By placing energy enhancements in these areas, you can intentionally bring about profound results!

Fruit of the Womb

Mika and Mark wanted to have a baby, but were having no success becoming pregnant. The delay had them frustrated and bewildered.

It was the second marriage for both and Mika's biological clock was ticking. They had financial stability and a house ample enough to hold several children. They were tired of well-meaning relatives and friends asking them when they were going to start a family. In fact, whenever someone brought it up, Mark would curtly reply, "We're having as much sex as possible!"

One of Mika's friends introduced the couple to me, and Mika invited me to come to her home for a feng shui consultation. She showed me around, stopping at the room where the couple planned to put the nursery. Currently it was a guest bedroom and a "put-the-stuff-you-don't-know-what-to-do-with-yet" room. This room contained a mishmash of items that had no "home" anywhere else. However, the room was auspiciously located. When we examined the layout of the entire house, we found that the planned nursery serendipitously happened to be in the bagua zone of Children and Creativity.

I suggested that Mika wait no longer, but immediately begin transforming the guest bedroom into a nursery that would be a sanctuary for a child. While I was there we started to remove extraneous things. The next step was to cleanse and sanctify the room, so we did a ritual in which we burned sage and rang bells. Next, we brought artwork, stuffed animals, and other child-like items, such as toys and baby books, into the room.

Looking at the room's bagua (remember, the map can overlay a home, room, or smaller surface), we saw that the dresser that was already there had coincidentally been placed in the Children and Creativity zone. This was where we would build an altar for fertility and to honor the energy of children. On the altar, Mika and Mark put photos of their nieces and nephews. They also added living plants, white candles (the color that enhances the energy of Children and Creativity), a small bowl of ripe fruit to symbolize the ripeness of Mika's womb, and other symbols that were personally resonant. The couple had acquired a few baby items in the early stages of trying to get pregnant. Some of these were added to the altar as well.

When we finished furnishing the room and building the altar, we stood in front of the dresser, lit the candles and incense, and then prayed aloud, directly to the couple's baby "waiting in heaven," as if he or she were already a living being. We asked the baby to come to Mika and Mark. Before I left, I encouraged Mika and Mark to continue to *attend to the altar, regularly adding to it and praying and meditating. It's important to focus often on a desired outcome when you build an altar with a specific intention in mind. Remember: Where attention goes, energy flows. Because there was still a guest bed in the room, I also suggested that they spend intimate time there.*

Four months later, I got an excited telephone call from Mika. She was delirious with baby bliss! Seven months later she gave birth to their daughter, Stephanie.

Communing With Your Sacred Space

A Dialogue With Your Sacred Space

A dialogue can help you access the psychological entity of the room you've chosen—its "personality" and "soul." On an energetic level, your planned sacred space has its own needs and desires. This activity is also an opportunity to explore your current emotional, mental, and spiritual connections to the area you've selected and discover its hidden meaning.

While your entire home is a reflection of your whole being, by itself each room is a reflection of only a few aspects of your life. The image it reflects depends on the activities the room contains and the types of relationships it nurtures, as well as how you handle these. Therefore each room has a different story to tell you about how it feels and relates to you. By learning to read the symbols your room holds, you can determine what is working well and working poorly, and the ways the room needs to be modified and enhanced. Some spaces support us and some sabotage us, yet we are the ones who arrange and maintain them. As you work through this dialoguing process, you will begin to understand more about how your interactions with your home contribute to your overall well-being and the potential manifestation of your intentions.

Start by getting out a pen and paper. For the purpose of this explanation, I have chosen the living room area of the home, but the same process would work in any area. You should set aside a good stretch of time for this activity, perhaps as much as an hour.

Sit down on your sofa or favorite chair and get comfortable. Close your eyes and breathe deeply. Take a few minutes to quiet your mind. When you feel completely relaxed, slowly open your eyes.

Now, begin writing a letter to your living room. Start with any salutation or endearment that comes to mind, such as *Dear Living Room*. You are going to write as though your living room has a personality and presence. Write as if you've known each other for a long time, but you haven't had an opportunity to sit down and have a really good conversation in ages.

First, tell your living room all the things that you love and cherish about it. When I did this exercise, I can remember telling my living room how much I loved its coved ceilings and the wonderful Tuscan-like yellow wall color.

Then, tell it all the things that bother and annoy you about it. When I was writing this part of my letter to my living room, I explained that I didn't like the seemingly endless amount of dust bunnies that it accumulated and the sticky residue on the hardwood floors that occasionally seeped out from the indoor plants.

Allow your eyes to move around the room and linger whenever they fall upon something that is pleasant or unpleasant. Then write it down.

Let your writing be a conscious free-flow of expression. There are no grades here, no good or bad aspects to what you feel about your space. No one is going to read this letter except you. It's only a process to bring what is usually subconscious into your conscious awareness. You're just telling your old friend, your living room, how you feel. Share your likes and dislikes.

Next, apologize for how you may have treated it poorly from time to time. For instance, I apologized to my living room for having neglected the wooden floors. They needed attention and should have been refinished.

Then, thank it for its positive contributions to your life, such as comforting moments and pleasurable experiences. During parties and holidays, my living room exudes warmth and a friendly ambiance. This is an example of the kinds of happy experiences for which to express gratitude.

Reminisce about the good times and the bad times. Be sure to write them down.

If, as your eyes continue to move about the room, you notice an object or a piece of furniture, such as the fireplace, feel free to let your creative conversation speak directly to that element. Tell the fireplace what you think or feel about it. Is there a special painting or collection of items arranged on a table? Include them. When you begin to look around at and talk to your living room, you'll probably find an endless number of topics to discuss.

This is important: Tell your sacred space what you would like it to become. Tell it your hopes, wishes, and desires. Specifically describe how you want it to feel and how you want it to support you and your intentions. Be as clear as possible about expressing the ways it could nurture your soul.

The first half of the dialogue usually takes somewhere between 15 minutes and one hour to complete. Simply let it last as long as it takes to allow your heart to speak to your room. Try to set aside your judgments and preconceptions.

When you feel that you are finished with the letter, take a moment to thank your room for sharing in your life. Then take a deep breath, get up, and move around. Stretch your arms and legs, walk around a bit, and drink a glass of healthy, pure water or juice.

Now, when you are ready again, come back into the same room and pick a *different* place to sit. This is important. In the second half of this activity, your *room* will be speaking directly to you, thus it is vital that you sit somewhere other than where you were sitting when *you* were speaking *to* the room. You might also want to light a scented candle, burn some incense, or make a fire in the fireplace. The room will respond energetically to your attentiveness.

As previously, sit comfortably and begin to breathe slowly and deeply with your eyes closed. When your body and mind are relaxed and calm, and with your eyes still closed, imagine the "personality" of your sacred space. Feel its presence and energy come alive. Sense its essence and soul. I guarantee that it has much to share with you.

Be gentle and patient. Your room has never had such an open opportunity to speak to you before. Its attempts to speak to you in the past have been couched (no pun intended!) in subtle innuendoes and unspoken hints. As this may be its first chance to communicate and be acknowledged, the room may be shy initially, perhaps even untrusting. Your tenderness and love make it safe for the room to reveal its secrets.

Now, slowly open your eyes and begin a new letter from your room to yourself: *Dear [insert your name]*.

This part of the exercise, much like the first part, could take only 15 minutes. It is more likely, however, that it will take longer. I obviously don't know what your sacred space will share with you, but I'm certain you will be amazed about what it has to say.

If you feel that you are having some difficulty getting your room to open up to you, ask it some open-ended questions, such as:

- How do you feel about the ways my family and I generally use you?
- When do you feel most loved?
- When do you feel most misunderstood?
- What do you want most of all from us? me?
- Why are you important?
- What do you like?
- What do you dislike?
- How can you support my intentions?

A very important criterion here is always to let the room know that it is loved and you are completely open to it freely sharing its feelings with you. This time is for you to only listen and hear. Offer no rebuttal, debate, or response. Your space may have some upsets, disappointments, and anger. Just allow it to have its "say." Sometimes, being allowed to express an upset will dissipate the feeling and heal the upset.

As before, when you are finished listening to your room and writing down the messages, take an opportunity to thank the room for sharing with you. You might also promise your room that in the future you will try to be a better listener.

Finally, ask your room if it has anything else it would like to share with you. If not, send it loving and caring thoughts and say good-bye for now. Close your eyes again and take a few deep breaths. Stretch and come back to yourself.

If possible, go for a nice walk around the block, down the street, or to the park. Just get outside of the house and into the fresh air. Let your inner and outer selves have a few minutes to integrate what's been revealed. When you return, notice how this dialogue has led you to a deeper emotional understanding of the room's personality, and reflect on the benefits and limitations you created (subconsciously or consciously) in the room. Perhaps it heals, loves, and uplifts you, or maybe it drains, dispels, and depresses you. To some degree, within each room in our homes, we display messages—usually subconsciously—that reveal who we are, what we do, and who we want to become.

A Final Thought

Sanctuaries, altars, and shrines can be created on many levels; therefore, it's easy to create a sacred space. You already have a personal vision of what your sanctuary would be like; you simply need to honor it. A sacred space provides a vehicle to the loving areas of the heart and the yearnings of the soul. As Joseph Campbell once wrote, "Your sacred space is where you find yourself, again and again." While there is no magic formula to discovering a location for sacred space, the techniques you have learned in this chapter should help you identify a good site.

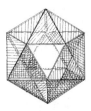

Chapter 2

Space Clearing and Sanctification

> "Each small task of everyday life is part of the
> total harmony of the universe."
> —George Eliot

*N*ow that you have chosen the spot for your sacred space, it is time to prepare it. The preparation process is like priming a canvas for a painting or plowing a field to sow crops; your home sanctuary is your masterpiece and the fulfillment of your intentions is your intended harvest. You can use the techniques in this chapter whether you are planning to create an entire sacred room or garden, or simply planning to place an altar or shrine within a specific area.

There are usually several steps involved in space clearing. You will begin by uncluttering and physically cleaning the space. Then you'll use one or more clearing methods to release old patterns of energy and circulate stagnant chi, thus establishing a more positive flow. Space clearing indoors and outdoors has slight differences, however the fundamentals are the same—and we'll discuss both kinds. Finally, you will sanctify this freshly cleansed space so that it can support your intentions and nourish your activities. Sanctification is a blessing that encourages harmony and prosperity. Every step of the way, you will also work with your own personal energy to anchor it into the space.

Because the area you are planning to devote to sacred activity may be large or small, and because you have your own style of doing things, you may need to set aside only a few hours for preparation or you may need to set aside a weekend or a whole week. Take whatever amount of time you need to be deliberate and honor your spiritual essence. Most people find that they continue to modify their sacred space over the long-term, adding refinements and new dimensions as their lives progress and unfold. The advice that follows will get you started, but you can always refer to it later.

Cleaning House

Simplify, Simplify, Simplify

Clearing your clutter is a fundamental feng shui practice. It is not a good idea to enhance the energy of a space filled with watered down or stagnant energy from possessions that hold unpleasant or difficult memories. Clutter can be an obstacle when bringing your new intentions into existence. To create a powerful future for yourself, you need to get rid of anything from your past that is literally or symbolically holding you back. When you're feeling stuck in your life, this particular step can help blast through any obstructions, which is what happened to my friend Roger.

Roger had an accumulated lifetime of "stuff" in his house. He was a real estate agent, but lately sales were down and he was barely making ends meet. In addition, he was always in a tizzy. Amidst plenty of drama, he was never able to catch up on all his projects, relationships, or responsibilities. I had done a feng shui consultation at his home a few years earlier and recommended that he clear out most of his stuff. After a divorce he had moved into a smaller home without getting rid of any furnishings. His belongings now filled up every room—including the garage—floor to ceiling.

One day we ran into each other. "Have you decluttered yet?" I asked him. Fortunately, he had recently hired a professional organizer. He told me that this young man had traveled from Los Angeles to Santa Barbara for four consecutive days and worked with Roger on his house from 8 a.m. until 10 p.m., breaking only for meals. He was intuitive, passionate about his work, and tireless. The organizer empowered Roger, little by little, to remove everything from his home that wasn't loved or needed. At first it was difficult, painful, and challenging. But as they progressed, Roger felt giggly and upbeat. He began to find tremendous humor in the fact that he could relinquish so many old emotional attachments so quickly. In the end, his front yard was filled with more boxes, clothing, furnishings, and items than Roger knew he had.

What did this do for his feng shui? Literally, within three weeks of the thrift store coming and carrying away two truckloads of clutter, Roger had more than $5 million of real estate in escrow. I know it sounds like magic, and maybe a little crazy, but it works.

◆ ◆ ◆

Go through the area that you have identified for your sacred space. Make time to clear out any clutter and to simplify your furnishings. Take a good look around. If you have identified an entire room, then go through its closets, cabinets, and drawers. Assess the energy of everything you find. Ask: Do I need this? Do I love this? If the answers are "no," get rid of it. Throw it away, give it away, or sell it.

Gather boxes, trust your instincts, and go for it. You will be amazed at how much easier this process becomes once you gain a little momentum. It's as though the more you have and the more you relinquish, the greater your results will be. You will notice a sense of physical, emotional, and spiritual release. And once accomplished, you will have "cleaned the slate" energetically and psychologically in your new sacred space.

Use Soap, Water, and "Elbow Grease"

Next, physically clean the area you intend to use for your sanctuary from top to bottom. If you are indoors, scrub, sweep, and polish! Remove cobwebs, dirt, and dust. Open the windows to allow any old, stale air and negative energy to be carried out and away on the breeze.

If you are outdoors, rake, sweep, and weed until your site is tended. In addition, declare your intentions out loud as you clean.

Purifying Yourself

Before you commence space clearing and sanctification, I recommend that you begin by preparing your own energy field for the task at hand. Your personal energy is a conduit to the life force of the universe, so it is vital to purify it before cleansing the energy of your new sanctuary. If you are "clogged up" in some way, such as by anger, your channels of intuitive communication are not as clear or receptive as they could be.

Human beings are a trinity of body, mind, and spirit operating as one unit. So, in order to cleanse your "psychic wiring," you must benefit from cleansing on all three levels. The first of these is your *body*. The day before you begin the clearing process, eat lightly or do a juice fast. I prefer to consume only steamed vegetables and fresh fruit or vegetable juices during this time. On the day of your space clearing and sanctification, take a long shower or bath. Bathing refreshes, renews, and lightens your energy.

Afterwards, take time to ponder your intention and meditate. Refer back to your notes from Chapter 1 about what you want for the sacred space and also the information you learned by holding a dialogue with the specific area that called out to you. When you are comfortably relaxed, listen to your inner voice whispering to you. Now, if you feel clear, centered, and otherwise ready, you may begin.

Space-Clearing Techniques

Space clearing is part of your journey of manifestation. Continue to focus on your intention as you prepare your sanctuary. Stay mindful and enjoy every moment.

So that you can work from a "clean slate," begin by moving everything possible out of the room or area you are going to use. Once you have done this, sit quietly and experience the energy of the chosen space for a while. Play music that relaxes you, and allow the moment to take you deeper within. Music has been used to induce transcendent states of consciousness since ancient times because it balances the body, mind, and spirit.

Then, perform one or more of the following space clearing techniques, using fragrant smoke, bells, clapping, holy water, drums, singing bowls, or gongs.

Two words of caution: Avoid space clearing when you are depressed or angry, as it will be counterproductive. Also avoid doing these rituals when you are pregnant or sick, as you do not want to absorb negative energy.

Smudging

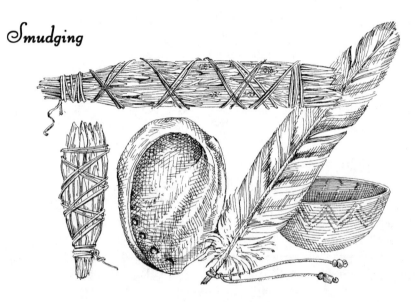

Smudging tools

Native Americans refer to the practice of using smoke for spiritual purification as *smudging*. Although many kinds of herbs, or incense, may be used in smudging, the most common are sage and sweet grass. Sage is used because of its ability to drive away negative spirits, while sweet grass, with its crisp aroma, is known to attract and amplify beneficial healing energy.

To perform a smudging ceremony in the space where you are going to place your sanctuary or altar, you will need the following tools:

- *A smudge stick or loose fragrant herbs:* Smudge sticks are bundled herbs that can be purchased at alternative bookstores, gift shops, and markets specializing in natural foods. You may also make your own smudge sticks using local, indigenous herbs.

- *A shell or bowl:* When you are holding and carrying burning smudge sticks or herbs, be sure to use a fireproof bowl or dish to catch any ashes, embers, or sparks. I prefer using an item from the natural world, such as an abalone shell, or a favorite piece of clay pottery. If your container is metallic, remember to have a hot pad nearby.

- *A feather:* As you engage in the ritual, it is particularly powerful to smudge with the use of a feather. Feathers are used to direct and manipulate smoke. They also have a powerful connection to the spirit world, and different animal feathers possess their own particular energy. Think about what you want to achieve before selecting the feather that you use. Follow your own intuition.

    I have two feathers that I like to use. One is a Canadian goose feather that I found in the Northwest. Because these geese migrate great distances, as a totem they're linked with togetherness, seasonal cycles, safe travels, and hope. The other feather I found in Kenya. My tour guide said it came from a vulture. As a totem, the attributes associated with the vulture are patience, justice, karmic protection, and healing. Other totemic birds will be discussed in Chapter 4, Gathering Ingredients and Power Tools.

    Caution: Bird feathers may carry disease if you find them in the wild. If you are concerned, disinfect the feather you pick up. Many spiritual stores carry nontoxic, natural feather wands for smudging.

- *Matches:* Matches are needed to light your herbs.

A SMUDGING RITUAL

As I mentioned, before clearing your space it is best to purify yourself. You've already taken a bath or shower, now you will cleanse your energy field. Afterwards, you may notice that you feel more balanced and centered and have a greater sense of clarity, which can assist you in smudging the space. Follow these basic steps:

To create smoke, carefully light the end of the smudge stick. Once you can see that the herbs are well ignited, blow out the flame. The herbs should continue to gently smolder. Either hold your lit smudge stick or keep the smoldering herbs in a bowl (preferable if you are using a feather).

Now, close your eyes and quietly center yourself. Ask your spirit guides and any special saints, angels, or masters to accompany your ritual.

Next, gently waft the smoke towards the top of your head using a feather or a cupped hand. Then bring the smoke towards your face, down to your chest, across both arms, and down the center of your body to each leg in turn. While you are doing this, imagine that all your thoughts, feelings, and emotions are being washed clean, healed, and replenished with love and joy.

When you have smudged the front of your body, do the same, as best you can, with the back of your body. Gently waft the smoke with the feather or a cupped hand along the back of your head, down your spine, arms, and legs. Imagine the smoke lifting away any negative or harmful energy and allowing the beneficial energy of love to ignite your heart and soul.

If you have a partner, you can take turns smudging each other, front and back.

Now, to smudge your sanctuary, place the smoking herbs in the shell or bowl and hold the bowl in one hand. Hold the feather in your other hand. Then, using little flicks of the feather, begin moving the smoke lightly around the perimeter of the room or area. Work clockwise starting at the easternmost corner. You may invoke or pray as you smudge. Stay focused. Make sure to get smoke into every corner and nook. Reach up, as high as possible toward the ceiling, to energize the upper areas of the room.

When you have completed smudging, put down your smudge stick or burning bowl. Stand in the center of the room and ask the Divine to help complete the purification process. At this time, say a simple smudging prayer, such as:

"Mother, Father, Sister, Brother Spirit
Bring the energy of healing, love, abundance, and peace
To this altar (or sanctuary), this home, and this family.
For this and for all our blessings, we give thanks."

Better yet, make up a prayer of your own that allows your heart and soul to speak. This stage of your ritual is important because you want to imbue your sacred space with blessings and grace now that the energy has been cleared. Invoke the spiritual realms and ask for both support and gentle, positive energy to suffuse your sanctuary. Always end by offering your thanks.

A word of caution: When you have finished your smudging ceremony, be certain the herbs are completely extinguished. Even though they can appear to be out, they may continue to smolder.

Ryan's Hope

Ryan, a local Realtor and friend, called me to do a space-clearing ritual at one of his own homes, a property he had remodeled from top to bottom. He'd spent plenty of time and money re-landscaping the over-grown and neglected 2-acre site. He created a tranquil garden paradise with walking paths, gazebos, ponds, fountains, bird houses, a natural rock hot tub with cascading fountains, and several places to sit, contemplate, and entertain. Originally, he thought this would be his new residence. But rather than keep it, he decided to put it on the market. Now, for some reason, it wouldn't sell. Granted, he was asking top dollar—however, it was such a wonderful property and home that it certainly warranted his asking price.

Because Ryan was frustrated about the lack of interest from buyers, he requested that I visit the property as soon as possible. We scheduled a ritual for the next afternoon. It was a warm, sunny, summer day and I was working alone. I got out my smudging tools and my Tibetan bell and dorje. Then I started with a prayer and the intention to clear any negative or stagnant energy associated with the property for the purpose of sending it off to a new owner. I cleansed the garden and home, and also made mental notes of small feng shui cures he should apply here and there, paying particular attention to the zones that pertained to *Prosperity and Abundance*. These would be the most important areas to set the intention to sell the property.

When he arrived an hour or so later, Ryan went straight to work installing the feng shui remedies, which included hanging crystals and wind chimes in a corner of his garden where there was a wonderful Asian-inspired teahouse. In addition, I suggested that once a day, he light a candle and a stick of incense inside the gazebo and spend a few minutes visualizing the new owner happily and delightfully living in the house and enjoying the serene garden he had created. It was important for Ryan to make a formal gesture to let go of his attachment, as he had put so much time, effort, money, and love into the property. An energetic attachment can inadvertently keep a property from selling.

Well, he did it! About three weeks after the space clearing ritual, Ryan's home went into escrow at almost the full asking price.

Holy Water

Human beings have a primal connection to the oceans that spawned life on Earth and to the watery environment of the womb. We know that to survive and maintain health, we must drink water. When we cry, our tears heal us emotionally. Water is also a powerful tool for cleansing and sanctifying the energy of a sacred space. Like a shower of rain, it can purify and disperse negative chi, thus restoring clarity and harmony.

Holy Water, which has been blessed, is used in the sacred ceremonies of many religions. Followers of Christianity, for instance, believe they are returned to a state of Divine Innocence through the ritual of baptism. Many legends describe qualities bestowed by water, including life, youthfulness, and wisdom. The ancient Egyptians said that water birthed their gods. It is also felt that water, from springs located near sacred sites, has special healing properties. In feng shui, water is recognized as an elemental force of *creation*. It represents the bagua zone of Journey and Career.

A WATER SPRINKLING RITUAL

For this space clearing ritual, you will need holy water. You may use water that comes from a church or a temple (many make this available to followers), or you may personally bless the water by calling upon any deity or deities, angels, or spiritual guides that feel appropriate to you and asking that your intention be supported.

Begin by lighting a candle in the middle of the room.

Sprinkle the holy water around the room, slowly walking in a clockwise fashion. You may want to use a small branch, or favorite flower, to sprinkle the water.

When you are done, take a moment to offer your gratitude.

Alternatively, you can mist or spray your space using water that has been energetically "charged" by the sun, moon, or crystals. This creates an environment rich in negative ions, similar to being near a waterfall or an ocean. When I'm unable to use another method of space clearing, I often use an atomizer filled with holy water and my favorite essential oil to spray my real estate office.

Bells and Tingshaws

From the earliest of times and throughout many cultures, the ringing of bells has been used both for protection and for summoning spirits and deities. Bells have been rung to call people to services in Western churches and synagogues. They are also common in temples in China, Tibet, and India. Vibrations from bells can disperse accrued stagnant and negative energy by influencing and increasing the flow of positive energy.

Physicists tell us that all atoms, molecules, and subatomic particles are constantly moving and shifting in a resonating, vibrating pattern of inaudible sound—a natural, organic, cosmic harmony of vibration. That's why the sound of a bell affects the energy fields of all animate and inanimate objects.

Here are a few kinds of bells you might use:

*   *Silver bells:* These have a light, pure tone and are feminine, or yin, in nature. Silver is associated with the moon and the mystical realms of the night.
*   *Balinese bells:* These are considered some of the finest bells you can use for space clearing and sanctification.

The Balinese offer prayers and rituals during the entire process of producing their bells, which adds to their exquisite quality and mystical energy.

- *Tibetan bells:* These are typically made from seven metals: iron, copper, tin, silver, lead, gold, and zinc. They usually come with a *dorje*, a small metal object used to strike them. In Buddhism, the hand bell symbolizes the feminine (yin), and the dorje represents the male principle (yang). They often are used together because they represent the yin and yang and the balancing of life forces. In conjunction, they symbolically create harmony out of the inner and outer paths to enlightenment.

- *Brass bells:* These generate a stimulating and vibrant energy and would be appropriate bells to use in the zone of Prosperity and Abundance.

- *Bronze bells:* These are very useful for grounding energy. They emanate a deep tone that gives you the feeling of being settled and centered.

- *Tingshaws:* Tingshaws are two, brass-like cymbals attached to each other by a leather cord that's approximately 10 inches long. When struck or tapped against each other, they resonate gently. For a sharper ring, strike them more strongly at an angle.

Bell, dorje, and tingshaws

CLEARING WITH BELLS OR TINGSHAWS

Begin by standing in the middle of the room. Ring your bell and notice the degree of clarity in the tone. How does it sound? Clear? Muffled? If you often use bells or tingshaws for clearing energy, you will begin to gain an ability to "hear" the different sounds from the bell. If the energy is old and stagnant, for instance, the ringing might sound heavy and muffled. If the energy of the space is hyperactive and filled with discord, the sound may be shriller. As you become accustomed to the use of bells, your ability to discern the tones of the energy in the rooms will improve.

Now, ring the bell strongly, listen to the tone to decipher the quality of the energy of the room. Ring the bell again before the previous tone completely diminishes. Do this several times until you are quite sure that the tone is clear and resounding.

As you continuously ring the bell, slowly walk in a spiral that is gradually enlarging from the center. Keep spiraling and ringing until you are at the outer edges of the room. Just as in the smudging ritual, walk in a clockwise manner.

If the sound in the room still sounds muffled, feels heavy, or isn't clear, repeat the spiral until the sound of the ringing is resonant and strong. Pay particular attention to corners, nooks, and the areas around large pieces of furniture.

Finally, come back to the middle of the room. Invoke your intentions, send out loving prayers, and bless the room with your personal energy.

Gongs and Singing Bowls

Gongs and singing bowls are potent power tools. The resounding energy that emerges from them lingers long after you stop hearing their sounds. If you are shopping for a bowl or gong, listen intently to their tones. Choose the one that speaks to you on a deep level.

Although the use of gongs dates back to early Asia, you can find them now in many shapes and sizes. Hanging gongs create a mesmerizing tone when struck with a wooden mallet wrapped on one end with leather. Large hanging gongs, with a platter-shaped piece, can be used to clear the energy of your entire home or room. Smaller, handheld gongs are nice for clearing the energy of an altar or shrine. Strike the gong with the mallet and allow the reverberating tone to encompass the room as you circle it.

Singing bowls are thought to have originated in the regions of Tibet, Nepal, and northern India. When properly used, they create a very powerful soul-touching sound and vibration. This technique can not only cleanse the energy of your sacred space, but can sanctify it as well. Two types of singing bowls that are most often used are those that are made from a mixture of metals and those that are quartz crystal. Both types produce an amazing and intoxicating mixture of sound, vibration, and energy. Treat your bowls with care and respect and they will honor you in return.

A Tibetan or Nepalese tradition is to use a metal bowl on which you run a mallet around the inner (or outer) edge to create a tone that builds in intensity and volume. The bowl must remain stationary to gain full volume. Singing bowls can clear and invoke energy at the same time. Negativity and stagnant energy is whirled away while a sacred tone attracts a deluge of luminous cosmic energy into the home.

For space clearing, you could first place the singing bowl in the center of your room and then move it to a few other locations. Remember to invoke your intentions.

Drums

Usually our thoughts and minds are so swamped with information that we have difficulty sensing what is important or what has true meaning. But the primal sensation we get when we are mesmerized by the beat of a drum is directly sourced from our first experience of life: our mother's womb. This is part of the reason that the sound of the drum is so resonant with us. Drumming allows us to experience the sacred through non-verbal channels. Research shows that the act of drumming with both hands has the ability to synchronize the hemispheres of the brain. In most tribal cultures, Shamans, medicine people, and elders use drums to clear and stimulate energy.

Varieties of drums

In her books, *Space Clearing* and *Sacred Space*, Denise Linn powerfully shares her methods of drumming for space clearing. She explains that it is best to start out with a clear focus on your intention. Greet and acknowledge your drum by holding it near to your heart and sending it loving energy. Think about your intention. Are you creating a shrine to honor loved ones, a healing altar to help a friend in need, or a sacred space to practice your spiritual exercises?

While playing, sink deep into the essence of your drum and allow its own rhythm to arise. Denise explains that if no rhythm emerges on its own, you can begin with a gentle two-beat, pause, two-beat pattern, like the beating of your own heart.

Walk the perimeter of the room, as you learned in the method of cleansing known as smudging. Like the clapping exercise, you may notice that the drumbeat may sound muffled in certain areas of the room where the energy is negative or stagnant. Stop and remain in those areas until the sound from the drum is more and more clear and crisp. Allow the drum's own natural rhythm to emerge as you proceed.

Clapping

You can duplicate the space clearing procedure for ringing bells by simply clapping your hands. Clapping is always available to you if you don't have access to any other power tools for cleansing. Similar to the smudging method, move clockwise, starting from the eastern-most corner of the room. Begin low and move higher. Clap crisply from the floor to the ceiling, beginning your clap with widespread arms.

As with the bells, you will notice if the sound is muted or if it is crisp. Keep clapping until you hear a clear, crisp clap! Take a moment to invoke your intention and be grateful.

Be sure to wash your hands thoroughly afterwards.

Sanctification

There is a fine line between *cleansing* and *sanctifying*. In my own mind I make the following distinction: We *cleanse* a space to remove, release, and purify stagnant and negative energy; we *sanctify* a space in order to attract beneficial energy and good fortune. The word *sanctify* is defined as "to set apart as holy; to consecrate." Thus sanctification truly makes our spaces sacred.

When you have finished with cleansing the area, you can sanctify your sacred space in any number of ways. Here are some simple suggestions:

- ✦ Say a prayer. Ask Spirit to bless your sacred space.
- ✦ Light a candle (or several) and offer thanks.
- ✦ Light incense or burn resins to purify the area.
- ✦ Open the windows and doors to the fresh air and sun.
- ✦ Place a bowl of fresh fruit or a vase of flowers in the room.
- ✦ Sprinkle holy water while focusing on your intention.

In Chapter 9, you'll find other rituals you may want to implement for your sanctification ritual. As I will tell you frequently throughout this book, you are held back only by your imagination. The process can be as elaborate or as simple as you like. You can make the area sacred from a spiritual perspective with candles, incense, holy water, and prayers, or from a fun perspective you can make it a family event and throw a tablecloth of the floor and celebrate your new sacred space with pizza, sodas, and ice cream.

A Final Thought

You are learning feng shui, the art of working with physical objects on the material plane in order to make changes in the intangible plane of energy, which is always filled with possibility, light, and positive life force. Within this discipline, the process of space clearing and sanctification are acts of conscious creation. We are making a place to build a brighter future, manifest our intentions, and fulfill our desires.

Feng Shui Energy Enhancements

"I am awake."
—The Buddha

Y ou have decided to honor the needs and desires of your soul by creating home sanctuaries that nurture you and support the manifestation of your intentions. So far, you have identified the spaces in your home and garden that call to you for sanctification. By interacting and speaking to these rooms and areas, you have empowered spaces that you perhaps hadn't noticed before, and also acknowledged those that have been nourishing you, even when you didn't realize it! In the last chapter, you began the task of cleansing the energy of your surroundings. Now you are ready to build a sacred sanctuary, altar, or shrine and begin directing the positive flow of the life force in your surroundings.

Before you go into action gathering power tools and ingredients for your sacred spaces, or designing the rituals that will accompany your altars and shrines, let's take a look at ways to amplify and improve the ambient energy. Many of these feng shui energy enhancements are related to the five senses. They include the use of color, light, sound, scent, and nature. Some are tangible, and others intangible. Pleasing the senses provides comfort, joy, contentment, and peace. Feng shui holds keys to the beneficial placement of furnishings, decorations, and energy enhancements. Placement touches our "sixth sense," the subtle intuitive knowing of what *feels* comfortable and supportive.

Your Home and Life in Balance

Feng shui recognizes that everything in the world falls into the two archetypal categories of *yin* and *yang*. They are the major opposing forces from whose interactions the entire world is created. *Yin* is the ultimate feminine principle. *Yang* is the ultimate masculine principle. They are often depicted by a circle that is half dark and half light, but with a small spot of the other quality placed in each half to represent a seed that gives birth to the opposing principle. For could we feel cold if we could not feel hot? Could we feel tired if we could not feel energized? Could we feel roughness if we could not know smoothness? Would there be dark without light? Both are essential and interdependent.

In feng shui, the natural world is considered the manifestation of a divine balance of yin and yang that gives rise to physical health and every other form of well-being, from love and joy to abundance. Therefore feng shui attempts subtly to duplicate divine balance in our homes by equalizing their yin and yang qualities. Balance is seen as the harmony of many different kinds of polarities. Since the outer and the inner worlds are always reflections of each other, it is understood in feng shui that when we change the balance of yin and yang in an environment, our personal balance will also change, and vice versa.

Yin Qualities and Characteristics

- **Activities:** Yin is associated with resting and nurturing, so these would include meditating, sleeping, reading, and having a massage.

- **Sensations:** feminine, subtle, soft, open, receptive, dark, nurturing, cool, moist, subdued lighting, comfortable, loose, and a sensuous or peaceful ambiance.

- **Objects:** curving furniture, round or oval mirrors or picture frames, small windows, low ceilings, soft pillows and comfy fabrics, flowers and plants with rounded leaves, and quiet water features.

- **Colors:** subdued and muted colors, such as pastels, and dark and cool colors, such as black, charcoal, indigo, navy, or forest green.

- **Shapes:** curves and contours, oval, round, or irregular.

- **Gardens:** A shady spot under a tree, a contemplative area, a pond or reflecting pool, birdbaths, and low-lying meadows or valley-like areas of land.

- **Purposes:** Use predominately yin characteristics when you want to create a spa (either a home spa, day spa, or hotel spa), an altar or shrine for meditation or healing, a sanctuary for writing and journaling, a studio for creative endeavors such as painting or knitting, or a bedroom for a hyperactive child.

Yang Qualities and Characteristics

- **Activities:** lively gatherings, parties, playing children, dancing, singing, and anything upbeat.

- **Sensations:** hot, hard, bright lighting, sunshine, tight, sharp, quick, stimulating, loud, precise, and aggressive.

- **Objects:** bright lights, TVs, electronic equipment, games, computers, angular objects, pets and items that depict animals, large windows, and high ceilings.

- **Colors:** warm, strong, and bright colors, such as those in the spectrum of red, yellow, orange, and gold.

- **Shapes:** straight and tall, narrow, long, sharp, angular, and rigid, with hard lines.

- **Gardens:** a warm sunny area, a swimming pool or a large, splashing fountain, and a mountainous or hilly area.

- **Purposes:** use predominately yang characteristics when you want to create a children's play area, a busy recreation room, a hobby center, a thriving business office, or a fitness room.

Balancing the qualities of the feminine (yin) and the masculine (yang) in your sacred space will be one of the keys to enhancing its feng shui energy. This is usually done by combining attributes from both sides of the polarity. However, when you want to create a space to complement a special purpose, you can place more yin or yang energy in it.

An Extrovert and an Introvert Marry

Paul and Laurel had recently married and were in the process of combining their two homes, which were very different. Paul's home had predominately yin, or feminine characteristics and Laurel's had predominately yang, or masculine characteristics. Before making a final decision of where to start their new life together, they sat down and made lists of what they most and least liked about each home and held a conversation.

Paul had enjoyed a lifestyle by the sea. He'd been living in a weatherworn beach cottage with dark gray clapboard siding. Inside, it had pine walls and floors. The furnishings were a casual combination of throw rugs and comfy chairs covered in blue denim. His windows had many small, divided panes that looked out towards the water. He liked his home because he felt that he could relax and be cozy there. Laurel felt the same. She liked to hang out at Paul's so they could be romantic and intimate.

Laurel had been living in a sophisticated, contemporary townhouse in a small condominium complex. It had stucco walls covered with vines and a red-tiled roof. The inside was an off-white color, left as it had been painted when it was originally built and sold to her. Most of her home was also carpeted in an off-white color. It featured high ceilings and large windows, allowing for an abundance of light. Paul liked Laurel's place, because they seemed to have such a great time whenever they threw a party. She also preferred hers whenever they were hanging out with friends.

Ultimately, Paul (a smart young man) told Laurel that he wanted her to decide. He would be happy with whichever home she chose. Laurel (smart girl) decided that she would like to move into Paul's beachside cottage. She treasured the intimate yin energy it exuded, a perfect place to live as a cozy twosome. She knew it was important for their "sacred space" to support that essence, or feeling more than any other.

The 5 Elements

In feng shui, it is recognized that everything in the world is a combination of five elements found in nature: Wood, Fire, Earth, Metal, and Water. Each element represents specific attributes of chi, such as color, shape, direction, and mood, and has numerous other associations. For instance, Wood represents upward growth and progress. Fire represents heat and expansion. Earth denotes stability and dependability. Metal represents strength. Water is symbolic of fluidity and movement.

There are two basic ways to use the five elements in your sacred space. The first way is to balance them. As previously illustrated, balance creates harmony, health, and clarity. Clarity is essential to focusing and energizing your intentions. If you were to take notice of the places where you feel the most relaxed and comfortable, you would likely discover that the spaces that feel best hold the five elements in balance. In places that feel uncomfortable and disturbing, one element tends to outweigh the others.

The second is to draw upon their different qualities to exert specific influences on an environment. Once you clearly understand the energy of the five elements, you can harness their productive forces and avoid their negative potentials. This makes them a wonderful energy enhancement when you are transforming a sacred space and your life.

Wood

The Wood element is associated with the tree. In the natural world, the tree is associated with both heaven and earth, as it is firmly grounded by its roots, giving it stability. But it is also growing and expansive, reaching its branches to the skies. Many ancient cultures revered trees and considered them sacred. Wood can be pliant and bending like a vine, or sturdy and firm like a redwood. When the Wood element is in balance in your sacred space, it can enhance the energies of creativity, cooperation, and innovation. If there is too much Wood present, your creativity can feel blocked, overwhelmed, or stuck. Wood is a good energy enhancement when you want to symbolize new growth and new beginnings.

You can incorporate the Wood element in your sacred space through:

- Items made of wood, such as figurines and carvings.
- Wood building materials and furnishings, such as chairs, cabinets, and tables.

- Trees, plants, shrubs, and flowers, both natural and manmade.
- Organic and natural materials and fabrics, such as cotton or hemp.
- Textiles depicting flowers, leaves, or plants.
- Art pieces representing gardens, landscapes, flowers, and trees.
- Shapes resembling a tree trunk, such as poles and columns.
- Green colors, such as forest green, kelly green, lime green, celadon, and sage.

Fire

The Fire element can enhance the energy of your sacred space by increasing passion and enthusiasm. Fire is hot and stimulating. When there is just the right amount, you will boost the energy of your sacred area. But be forewarned, if you have too much Fire, your space can become "too hot to handle" or your emotions may run "hot and heavy." When your space is too fiery you may also find yourself feeling "hot under the collar."

Attributes of the Fire energy are found in:

- Art, objects, or figurines that represent the sun or fire.
- Art, figurines, or fabric that depict animals or people.
- Living animals, such as pets or the wildlife, around your home.
- Things made from animals, such as leather, fur, or feathers.
- Shapes that suggest pyramids or cones.
- Items that represent fire and light, such as the sun, bright lighting, fireplaces, candles, and electronic equipment of all kinds, such as TVs and computers.
- Colors such as red and orange.

Earth

The Earth element represents stability and grounding. Earth energy can be a foundation for creating anything you need to be safe and sound. It boosts patience and is associated with planning and step-by-step follow-through. With the right emphasis, it is secure and stable. But if it is too wet, it becomes slippery or muddy, throwing you off-balance, or giving you the sense of being "stuck." If it becomes too dry and hot, then it can be soft, shifting like sand or a blowing dust storm making it impossible to see clearly.

To increase the Earth energy of your sacred area, use the following sources:

- Anything made from adobe, bricks, stucco, or natural tiles.
- Ceramics, such as objects d'art, figurines, vases, and tableware.
- Earthenware pottery.
- Art, tapestries, or textiles featuring deserts or canyons.
- Square or rectangular shapes.
- Colors such as brown, earth tones, yellow, ivory, and rust.

Metal

When the Metal element is in balance in your space, it can increase your business and financial success. Metal is symbolic of coins and gems. If you are creating a shrine for prosperity or simply want to increase the energy in your home office, add more of the Metal element. But take care. If your space holds too much Metal energy, this can result in conflict and disruption. Metal also has the resonance of armor and weaponry.

To magnify the Metal energy of your space, find its attributes in these sources:

- Actual metals, such as gold, silver, brass, copper, chrome, steel, pewter, and aluminum.
- Stone surfaces such as marble, flagstone, travertine, limestone, granite, river rock, and concrete.
- Natural rocks, stones, boulders, and pebbles.
- Precious gems, gemstones, and crystals.
- Art and sculpture made from metal or stone.

- Moving metal objects such as wind chimes, mobiles, and clocks.
- Circular and oval shapes.
- Colors such as white, gold, silver, brass, and pastels.

Water

The Water element represents emotions, communication, learning, and travel. Water can nurture you like a morning mist, revitalizing and nourishing your mind and body with beneficial ions. Or it can be draining and uncontrollable like a furious rainstorm. Using the right amount of Water to balance your space can boost your intentions involving travel or studies, as well as your emotional relationships.

You can find the Water element in the following items:

- Objects and surfaces made of reflective glass, such as mirrors, prisms, cut glass, and crystal.
- Natural bodies of water such as oceans, lakes, and rivers.
- Manmade water features, such as swimming pools, ponds, fountains, and fish bowls or tanks.
- Art that depicts bodies of water such as oceans, lakes, and rivers.
- Free-flowing shapes.
- Dark colors, including black, charcoal, and navy blue.

An Elemental Quintet in Perfect Harmony

Alan was referred to me when he was considering listing his home for sale. Immediately upon arrival, even before I walked through the door, I was struck by a warm and embracing ambiance. He had an overgrown, natural garden strewn with a large array of statues of deities, fairies, butterflies, and Tibetan prayer flags that stopped me short. And there he found me, mesmerized and communing with the energy. He was easygoing and comfortable and we hit it off immediately.

When he led me inside again, I was infused with extremely pleasant and nurturing energy. His home exuded a sense of sacred space.

Why was that, I wondered? As we moved around, I could see that he had intuitively created a powerful balance of the five elements. For the Water element, he had several indoor water fountains, one right at the entrance—a very auspicious placement. Although most of his furnishings were darkly colored, there was a proliferation of cut glass in every room and prisms were hanging in the windows, sprinkling colored rays of light throughout his home.

The Metal element was mixed in by way of several large brass statues of Buddha and other deities. On top of a piano, there was also a large, golden reclining Buddha. He had also placed crystals, such as amethyst, citrine, and rose quartz, on various tabletops and windowsills. There were many metal candleholders filled with white candles. I also noticed Earth element features, such as a brick fireplace, stucco walls, and earth tone colors of the furnishings. Alan had collected antique earthenware pottery from all over the

world. There were many ceramic figurines of various gods and spiritual symbols situated around the house.

The Fire element was the most subdued, although held in equal balance. It was obvious in the candles and the fireplace, which was the focal point of the living room, as well as the small accents of red scattered here and there. He had also put photographs of his friends and spiritual masters throughout the house, representative of his inner Fire. And his black lab, Smokey, and huge cat, Jake, held court in the living room.

Representing the Wood element, there were a number of indoor plants, trees, and vases of flowers, in addition to the color green. The entire house had hardwood floors, and most of the furniture—the piano, tables, chairs, and cabinets—were made of fine woods. Alan was embarking on a second career that combined photography and computer graphics, and many of his best pieces depicted gardens and ponds with lotus flowers!

Color

You can enhance and magnify the energy of your sacred space, altar, or shrine by choosing colors that correlate with your intention or with a specific area of the bagua. If you want to foster creativity, for example, because you are planning to use your sacred space for writing or painting, you may work with the colors yellow and white. Yellow is known to stimulate intellectual pursuits and innovative thinking, while white is associated with the bagua zone of Children and Creativity. In this case, you might arrange yellow daffodils in a vase or light a white candle to attract those kinds of energy.

Throughout history, color has been used as a therapeutic and evocative medium by many cultures, including the Chinese and ancient Egyptians. They understood that color nourishes and influences the field of energy around us. Today, color therapists have also gathered evidence that the body and mind respond to colors. Warm colors, such as red, orange, and yellow, tend to be stimulating, and cool colors, such as blue and green, tend to be calming. So, on a physiological and psychological level, color affects how we act and how we feel, thus creating a significant impact on our lives.

Colors are also often associated with specific thoughts, feelings, and emotions, such as the concept of "feeling blue" when you're sad. It is important to recognize that different cultures have different associations to colors. For instance, in China—and in respect to feng shui—the color blue is associated with wisdom, introspection, and inner knowledge. The color white, most often associated with purity and innocence in the West, is associated with death in the East.

Because the meanings of colors varies from culture to culture and age to age, you should always remember to choose colors that resonate with you and how you want your sacred area to "feel." This may be highly personal. But if you are looking for guidance, or want to bring a certain intention into reality, try using the colors associated with the zones of the bagua to foster and heighten the energy of your chosen space.

- ◆ **Red:** The color of passion, romance, power, activity, excitement, and fame. Red brightens, uplifts, and stimulates energy. Be careful of decorating an entire room in red, as it has tremendous energy. Use red on an altar to heighten your name in the community or to gain a promotion. Try sumptuous red fabrics, flowers, candles, and hearts. In feng shui, red is associated with the bagua zone of Fame and Reputation. It represents the element of Fire.

*   **Pink:** The color of unselfish love, pink is emotionally soothing. Pink creates a sense of comfort and nurturing. It is also known to alleviate depression and feelings of loneliness. Use pink on an altar to initiate a romance or to improve a relationship. In feng shui, pink is associated with the bagua zone of Marriage and Relationship.

*   **Orange:** The color of creativity, community, and confidence. Orange is warm, romantic, happy, sociable, and flamboyant. This is a great color for a dining room or family room and is wonderful for a birthday or holiday altar, such as on Thanksgiving and Halloween (All Saints Eve). Use orange candles, flowers, and fruits.

*   **Yellow:** Yellow stimulates the intellect and creativity. It is known to positively affect concentration and academic achievement. Because yellow uplifts and brightens mood it is good for a den or study, and for an altar or sanctuary to enhance creativity, especially for writers, academics, and artists. Use yellow flowers, wall color, and fabrics. Yellow is associated with the element of Earth.

*   **Green:** The color of healing, stability, nature, family, and wealth. Green has gentle energy, cooling and soothing, so it increases balance, and harmony. It is a good color for a healing altar or sacred space, or for a family shrine. Use a green velvet scarf or fabric as an altar cloth and arrange the photos of your living relations and ancestors on it. In feng shui, green is associated with the bagua zone of Family and Health. It represents the element of Wood.

*   **Blue:** Blue evokes feelings of peace and tranquility. It is the color associated with self-knowledge and spiritual devotion, and therefore appropriate for a sanctuary or sacred space that is used for meditation and prayer. In Christianity, blue is the color associated with the Virgin Mary. Try a rich,

deep indigo satin or velvet as an altar cloth for an inspirational altar. Blue is an attribute of the element of Water. In feng shui, blue is associated with the bagua zone of Self-Wisdom and Knowledge.

- **Purple:** The color of wealth, prosperity, and abundance. In the Christian faith, purple is associated with Advent, the season preceding the birth of Christ. In some cultures, it is considered the color of royalty. Purple also attracts the energy of spirituality. To attract prosperity and enhance spirituality, use sumptuous purple velvet for an altar cloth, adding purple candles and amethyst crystals. Paint the walls of your sanctuary in shades of lavender.

- **Brown:** Brown is the color of soil. It is relaxing and connects us to the earth. The color is associated with all aspects of Mother Nature, including both the plant and animal kingdoms. Because it is symbolic of growing roots and stability, it is a good color to use when "grounding" an intention. Brown represents the element of Earth.

- **Black:** This is a very powerful "non-color." Black evokes power, success, knowledge, and mystery, and is related to the "dark realms" of the inner world. Use this color sparingly, as too much can be overwhelming and depressing. In feng shui, black is associated with the bagua zone of Journey and Career. It represents the element of Water.

- **Gray:** The color gray is independent and self-reliant. In the negative, we use the term "gray area" when something is neither black nor white. It can be non-committal. If you have too much gray around, you may feel deprived of vital energy. Use it sparingly. Gray is associated with the bagua zone of Helpful Friends and Travel.

- **White:** White is the color of all colors combined. It is symbolic of purity, innocence, cleanliness, and refinement. It is also associated with the higher "light" of spirit and enhances spiritual attunement. Be careful of an all-white room, however, which could feel uncomfortable. Use white on a wedding altar. It is associated with the bagua zone of Creativity and Children and represents the element of Metal.

Color can be applied in countless ways to create your sacred space. If you are designing a sacred room, it is easiest to start with the wall color, then move on to other furnishings and decorative items. If you are building an altar, begin with the color of your altar cloth. Then you can choose the colors of your candles, gems, flowers, figurines, and symbols. In Chapter 4, we'll talk about the many varieties of ingredients that are available.

Use color to enhance your sacred space in any manner that resonates personally with you. Keep in mind that bright colors attract energy. So, if you are intending to manifest a job, relationship, or anything else in your life that you believe requires intense energy, think bright and vivid. On the other hand, pastel colors, such as peach, violet, coral, and pink are soothing. So, if you are designing a sanctuary for peace, prayer, and meditation, you may want to use subdued shades of blue, lavender, or rose. They will soften the energy of a room and enhance spirituality.

Light

It is no coincidence that light is a powerful energy enhancement. In the Book of Genesis, God said, "Let there be light: and there was light." In the Epistle of St. John, it reads, "God is light, and in Him is no darkness at all." We are acquainted with the expression, "I saw the light," which suggests having an epiphany or psychological wake-up call. Natural light is symbolic of the internal light of the soul, of our "enlightenment." It can dissolve stagnant energy and be a potent healing salve.

Light and bright objects that can enhance the energy of your sacred space include natural light, indoor lighting, mirrors, candles, and cut glass.

- **Abundant natural light** uplifts stale energy. So keep your *windows* clean!

- **Interior lighting** can brighten a dark area of stagnant energy and uplift ambient chi.

- **Mirrors** are a common feng shui enhancement, directing beneficial chi into your sacred space and sending negative chi away. They should be clean, without any decorative veins or small panes. Damaged, faded, or scratched mirrors should be avoided.

* **Candles** boost energy on several significant levels: the flame can provide elemental "fire" energy, the color can enhance the area of a bagua with which it is associated, a scented candle can heighten a romantic or contemplative mood, and the smoke can "deliver" a message to the heavenly realms.

* **Cut glass**, either faceted or round, can reflect positive chi or disperse negative chi.

Sound

As you learned in Chapter 2, sound is valuable in cleansing the energy of a sacred space. Since it both stimulates and raises the frequency of the ambient chi, it can also be used as an energy enhancement. But sound vibrates your body as well as the environment. Do a couple of quick experiments. Place a hand on your chest and hum, and you will feel it stirring. Or put a hand on the floor near a loudspeaker and feel it tremble from the bass rhythms. So, obviously vibrations have a physical impact. Even more interesting is how sound affects human brainwaves. Different frequencies can "entrain" the mind to be calmer or more alert. Thus sound makes a perfect adjunct to relaxation, meditation, and rituals.

Research has shown that music can slow the heart rate and breath rate, lower blood pressure, and alleviate muscular tension. Recorded music can set the stage when you want to establish a certain mood. Many CDs that promote different states of consciousness are now available. Beta brainwaves occur when we're awake and feeling sharp. Alpha brainwaves occur when we're relaxing or daydreaming. Theta brainwaves occur when we're in deep meditation, a state that also promotes physical healing. You could spend a lifetime discovering and listening to music that feeds and uplifts your soul.

Instruments are wonderful energy enhancers, which you'll learn more about in Chapter 4.

Wind chimes can be used to uplift energy, so they are good enhancements for stagnant corners, near windows and entrances, and on porches. They may be used to keep positive chi from running quickly down a long hallway and out through the door. But they are most beneficial outdoors, where they can activate the chi in a sacred garden shrine. It is said that elemental beings (e.g., fairies, elves, and gnomes) are attracted by the tones rising and falling with the breeze.

Scents

One of the more subtle ways of shifting the mood of your home and sacred space is through the use of different scents. Our sense of smell is so intimately connected to our emotions, in fact, that specific aromas can suddenly take us back to times and places in our lives that we have long forgotten. After I graduated from the University of Washington, I received a position with a research institute in Brazil. Nowadays, the fragrance of a certain plant, which also grows in Southern California near me, immediately returns me to Brazil and the memory of being outdoors after a rainfall. Each of us also has deep associations with scents that can evoke powerful emotions for reasons that are individual. Experiment with essential oils and incense as an energy enhancement.

Essential Oils

Aromatherapy is the ancient therapeutic art of blending essential oils. *Essential oils* are the undiluted, pure plant extracts that come from leaves, flowers, herbs, and fruits. Some are obtained by steam distillation; others are pressed out by mechanical means. It is said that they contain the spiritual energies of plants. While essential oils are sometimes used by direct application to the skin (under the guidance of a knowledgeable expert), in the practice of aromatherapy they are added to potpourri, candles, and other heated surfaces in tiny quantities so they may evaporate and be breathed in. Research shows that using essential oils in this manner helps promote physical and emotional well-being.

Caution: If you tend to be highly allergic, essential oils may not be appropriate for you.

The intense healing powers of essential oils have been recognized for millennia. Over 5,000 years ago, the Egyptians used cedar wood in their mummification processes. The Normans used botanical oils to

Essential Oils: Characteristics and Benefits

- **Bergamot:** Bergamot has a spicy citrus aroma. It is often used as an antidepressant and can uplift your mood.
- **Cedarwood:** Cedarwood has a woodsy forest aroma. It has a calm and soothing essence that is good for respiratory ailments. It is a delightful winter scent.
- **Eucalyptus:** Eucalyptus has a mentholated aroma. It is a mental stimulant and is used to fight colds, sore throats, and flu because it has antiseptic and anti-viral properties.
- **Lavender:** Lavender has a gentle floral aroma. It is perhaps the most commonly used essential oil because of its many beneficial properties. It is best known to ease irritability, depression, tension, and fatigue.
- **Lemon:** Lemon has a clean, citrus aroma. It can be relaxing or stimulating depending on the person. It is widely used in kitchens to give them an uplifting energy.
- **Orange:** Orange has a fresh, sweet citrus scent. Because it elevates moods and can improve outlooks, it is often used to combat anxiety and depression.
- **Peppermint:** Peppermint has a strong mint aroma. It is a blend that stimulates the intellect and is helpful in combating colds and flu symptoms.
- **Ylang Ylang:** Ylang Ylang has a sensuous floral aroma. It helps alleviate nervous anxiety, depression, insomnia, and high blood pressure. Because of its alleged aphrodisiac abilities, it is sometimes used in candles for the bedroom.

*A variety of aromatic
energy enhancements*

combat infections and deter lice. The ancient Greeks believed that scent was a means of communing with the gods, and they were adept at choosing scents to evoke moods. Today, aromatherapy allows us to access the healing powers of plants even if we don't have access to a garden or wild forest.

Although there are some synthetic aromatherapy products available, I strongly recommend using only *natural* essential oils. Synthetic products commonly cause allergic reactions, and, if they are aerosol products, can contain chlorofluorocarbons that pollute the environment and can damage your lungs. Need I say more? You should always store natural oils in a cool, dark place—or darkened glass bottles—to preserve their potency. Essential oils are sold at most health food stores and many spas and gift shops.

Here are some methods for using the powers of aromatherapy to enhance the energy of your sacred space or altar:

- **Scented candles:** Scented candles combine the powerful effects of a chosen scent with the symbolic and energetic qualities of a candle. Choose a scent and color that, when combined, will activate the intention you desire. For instance, a violet candle in a lavender scent will enhance a meditation room. A pink candle combined with ylang ylang is ideal for a romantic bedroom or an altar for finding romance.

- ◆ **Potpourri:** You can create homemade potpourri by adding a few drops of an essential oil to a bowl of flower petals, seashells, or pinecones. Place these bowls in your sacred spaces and on your altar to enhance their energy.

- ◆ **Vaporizers:** There are many varieties of vaporizers from which to choose. Vaporizer rings that can be placed directly on top of light bulbs are one excellent option. Simply add a few drops of essential oil to the ring and turn on the light to release the scent. Another vaporizer that is better for an altar top is a kind made of ceramic. Pour a few drops of oil on top and light a small candle below to release the scent. A third option is to place a votive candle under a bowl of water scented with essential oil.

- ◆ **Diffusers:** There are several kinds of diffusers on the market that you can purchase. They are easy to use and will fill your sanctuary with the scent of your choice. These are best utilized in small rooms or areas. Electric diffusers can scent a large area. One type has a fan unit that blows air through a fabric-like filter that you soak with your desired scent. Another kind has a tiny blower that emits the scent in the form of a light mist.

You only need to use a *few drops* of an essential oil at a given time, as they are *extremely potent*. Always trust your own feelings and inner voice. If a particular scent doesn't appeal to you, or it doesn't seem to resonate with the intention of your altar or sanctuary, then **stop using it**.

Incense

Fragrant herbs, gums, and resins have been burned during religious ceremonies throughout history, from the Buddhists and Hindus to the Christians. Originally, the scents symbolized the presence of spiritual power, while the smoke represented the prayers and needs of the worshipers, wafting skyward to the heavens, where the gods and goddesses lived. Are you familiar with the biblical story of the Magi (three kings carrying gifts of frankincense and myrrh to the baby Jesus)? That is an early mention of incense. Nowadays, Japanese incense is considered to be the finest, as it is blended with meticulous attention.

Incense and resin are easy to come by and to use, and they have powerful properties. Some incense comes in sticks, some in pellets or cones. You can choose from many kinds of flame-resistant containers in which to burn them: wooden, metal, and ceramic vessels of different shapes. The same health food stores and gift shops that carry essential oils will have the items you need. Experiment with fragrances of incense to suit your mood. I find that the scent that attracts me varies from day-by-day.

Nature

Whether you resonate with the mountains, the sea, wild woodlands, manicured parks, or the vastness of the desert, you can bring the sacred energy of natural places to life within your home sanctuary. Mother Nature's treasures are diverse, and the soul is nourished by exposure to these soothing and positive essences.

The sacred energy of life emanates nowhere more palpably than from animate aspects of the natural environment. Besides being aesthetically pleasing, trees, plants, flowers, fruits, animals, and birds are vibrantly infused with electromagnetic force and can literally awaken the life energy in your sacred space.

Living Plants, Flowers, and Fruit

Individual plants, terrariums, and potted flowers can amplify the energy of your sacred space. However, you must always ensure that plants on your altar or shrine are healthy and robust. Otherwise, they bring in deficient energy. Each species of plant carries its own particular energy. For instance, ferns have the ability to absorb and cleanse energy, thus bringing luck and protection. Strong, woody plants have a grounding effect. And if you enjoy the company of fairies and elemental spirits, the violet is the "queen of the fairy totems" according to Loren Crudden, a shaman, healer, and author of *The Spirit of Place*.

A bouquet of sunflowers suffuses a space with luck and prosperity and promotes "always looking on the bright side." Roses, which radiate love and beauty, make a stunning tribute on an altar to the Mother Goddess. The timeless lotus flower symbolizes transformation, enlightenment, and spiritual bliss. Daisies are fertility totems and would be a powerful addition to an altar dedicated to conceiving.

Fruit also carries tremendous life force. Bowls of fresh fruit are often found on altars of different kinds because fruit symbolizes health and well-being. Some people use them for healing altars, others for ancestral shrines to symbolize feeding those in the afterlife. Apples are said to represent good health, love, and immortality. Peaches symbolize friendship and joy. Oranges provide vitality and have an uplifting essence. Remember to use fruits that are in season, and are the kinds that you enjoy.

Pets

Domestic animals are associated with the Fire element and bring life force into any space where they reside. Dogs, known as "man's best friend," seem to enjoy their role as our companions and protectors and can be our daily link with the natural world. Their keen physical senses connect us with the realms of the subtle and unseen. Cats are sensitive to the spiritual realms and have been known to sense the presence of spirits. They are also good at sensing our moods. Years ago, if my children or I were ever sad and tearful, our cat, Taj, would mysteriously sense this, find us, and jump up on our laps to give comfort. Whenever I would meditate, she would sense that too (no matter where she was), find me, and jump up on my lap for a meditative snooze!

Birds heighten the energy of sacred space also. My friend, Geonine, has an African Gray Parrot named Spiro that exudes confidence and attitude. The bird is lively, funny, and can practically carry on a conversation. Spiro particularly likes children and can dissolve them into joyful gales of giggles at the drop of a hat. Another friend, Diane, keeps an immense cage in her family room that holds a number of lovebirds. Their soft cooing provides a warm, friendly mood for every gathering.

You'll learn about totemic animals and birds in Chapter 4, but here are a few insights: Lovebirds relate to good fortune, love, and contentment.

Canaries relate to thoughtfulness and self-expression and are known to uplift energy and delight. If you are fortunate enough to have a large pond with swans, they will enhance the energy of your garden with the qualities of transformation, wisdom, and grace.

Ritual Energy Enhancements

Ritual energy enhancements frequently involve using sacred diagrams to evoke benevolent forces for a specific purpose, such as healing and transformation. The sacred diagrams are symbols that link us to multiple levels of reality: the body, mind, emotions, relationships, the natural environment, and the spiritual realm. These include the medicine wheel, the labyrinth, and the mandala. Your participation and the participation of others during group work are the keys to unlocking sacred diagram power.

The Medicine Wheel

The Native American medicine wheel is a ritual energy enhancement that honors the six directions of nature—East, South, West, North, Sky, and Earth—which correlate to different aspects of human life. The East represents illumination and spirit, the South represents innocence and the body, the West represents introspection and the emotions, the North represents wisdom and the mind, the Sky is figurative of the Divine masculine, and the Earth is figurative of the Divine feminine. In addition, the medicine wheel pertains to the cyclical nature of existence: the seasons, days and nights, and the birthing and dying away of events, influences, and experiences in our lives.

Whenever you construct a medicine wheel, do so with respect, attentiveness, intention, honor, and gratitude. You can form the basic physical structure of the medicine wheel by making a circle of stones, on the ground or the floor, that has four spokes oriented to the four cardinal directions on the compass. Then you can place other ingredients upon it, such as written prayers, crystals, and mementos in order to "charge" them with its energy. Think of it as a focal point for praying and setting intentions. For the purposes of your sacred space, a medicine wheel can be any size. You can create a large one in your back lot or a smaller one on an altar. Remember that it is a vehicle both for drawing power inwards—attraction—and for radiating power outwards—releasing.

The elders of many cultures indigenous to North and South America have passed down specific ceremonies, rituals, and sacred formulas for medicine wheels. There are entire books on this subject that you should read to educate yourself more fully (see Bibliography). However, here is a basic explanation of how to create one:

Begin by smudging, or otherwise clearing, the energy of your stones (see p. 41). Also smudge yourself, any other participants in your ceremony, and the area where you are going to place the medicine wheel.

Native American Medicine Wheel

Next, place a stone at the center of your site and surround it with a ring of seven smaller stones. Some distance from these center stones—starting from the East, representing the sunrise and new beginnings—place four directional stones, going clockwise and aligning them with the compass points.

Then, set your "paths" or spokes, placing three stones from the center circle out to each cardinal direction.

Finally, using as many stones as you want, connect the outer directional stones with each other to create a curving perimeter.

Now your medicine wheel is ready to be used for a ritual, after you may be dismantle it or you may leave it in place.

Labyrinths

Labyrinths are similar in design to mazes, although the two differ because there is only *one* path through a labyrinth. Full of potent symbolism, they are associated with spiritual revelation. They represent both a journey to the center (each person's divine center, as well as the center of All That Is) and a return to the beginning. Drawings dating back to the Paleolithic Era have been found on cave walls that depict natural labyrinthine tunnels extending from the surface of the earth deep into the darkness underground. These were used for death and rebirth initiations, journeys into the symbolic (and real) shadow realms and back to the world and into the "light." Today, many people walk labyrinths as an act of contemplation. They are often built into cathedrals and established at retreat centers.

Like a medicine wheel, you can create a labyrinth of any size, depending on how much space is available. Outside in your garden, you could form a permanent and elaborate walking labyrinth by placing stones on the ground or by planting a boxwood hedge. On your altar, use small pebbles, shells, or beads and follow the path visually.

Placing a labyrinth in your sacred space can strengthen your intentions and your spiritual journey. It infuses your path with meaning and sacred energy.

Mandalas

Mandala is the Sanskrit word for "circle." It is a sacred diagram representing the cosmic life forces. In Eastern cultures, it is believed that universal energy holds patterns of vibration, which are represented, on the physical plane, by sacred geometric forms. Buddhists create mandalas for the purpose of meditation and enlightenment. Some are drawn or painted; others are three-dimensional. They can also be made in different sizes and with different materials.

In her book, *Feng Shui for the Soul,* Denise Linn states, "Using mandalas in the home is one of the fastest and most potent ways to activate life-force vitality and energy into a living environment." All you need to do is establish the center of a circle as a focal point and then surround it with objects associated with your sacred intention, such as healing or romance. Then, contemplate it often in order to enhance its resonance.

A Final Thought

Most of the energy enhancements that you've learned about in this chapter coincide with the fundamental principles and basic remedies of the traditional art of feng shui. You have also learned about energy enhancements that come from other wisdom traditions, such as labyrinths and Native American medicine wheels. Since there are so many kinds of "cures" to choose from, it helps to apply this rule of thumb: Only align your intention with enhancements that strongly resonate with your soul. You must love your sacred space and all that's in it. Also, even though it's tempting to incorporate almost every kind of enhancement, remember that simplicity is powerful. Sometimes less is more.

Now, go forth and have fun! You are ready to delight in discovering how balancing yin and yang, using the five elements, utilizing the bagua, accenting with color, and incorporating elements of nature, scent, and sound can be a joyous adventure in playing with the myriad of enhancements that can give your sacred space, altar, or shrine a glow of positive radiant energy.

Chapter

4

Gathering

Ingredients and

Power Tools

"*A private shrine can contain anything. Not necessarily religious,
but spiritual. If you define spirituality as that which connects
us most deeply to ourselves and to others.*"

—*Joan Borysenko*

*Y*ou have already chosen the location for your home or garden sanctuary, cleansed and sanctified it, and enhanced its ambient energy. The time has come to gather ingredients and power tools for the altars, shrines, and furnishing of this sacred space. Ingredients can include many different kinds of items, from altar cloths and religious icons, to crystals and mystical artifacts. They can be decorative, practical, symbolic, or all three. *Power tools* are ingredients, such as musical instruments and inspirational books, which are used during spiritual activities. In this chapter, I am going to guide you through many of the possible objects and images that are available, and help you understand how to work with them to fulfill your own special purposes.

When you are choosing your ingredients, please remember to select items that speak to your heart and your imagination. It is important that they reflect the vision of your sacred self and affirm your intentions. Remember, energy is subtle and intangible. It is not actually the physical objects you choose that are powerful, but the meanings and associations you assign to them. Any attraction you feel is a clue that certain objects or symbols are significant ones. If a particular object fills you with hope, joy, courage, or any other emotion you want to expand in your life, using that symbol as an ingredient can anchor the feeling in the space and in your life. Furthermore, when you focus your intention on an object, you instill it with energy. Then, even when you are not present, the energy of your intention will remain in motion. It is not necessary to fully understand why a symbol speaks to your soul. Simply embrace your feelings as you incorporate its qualities into your sacred sanctuary.

Altar Cloths, Tapestries, and Rugs

A beautiful fabric can be draped over a table or shelf and used as the basis of an altar or shrine. Fabric is symbolic of life. In Greek mythology, the fates wove individual destiny from many strands. It is also symbolic of human connection. African kinte cloth is said to have originated from the multicolored spools of thread belonging to seven brothers who had to learn to set aside their differences and cooperate. Fabric can also be the medium for wonderful imagery. Skilled artisans of many cultures create intricate tapestries and rugs, scarves, and textiles that tell stories or depict elements of nature, such as the Chinese who work with pure silk. Often, fabric serves both practical and expressive purposes. Natives of South, Central, and North America have a long tradition of blanket weaving that incorporates bold geometric designs.

Fabric has several qualities that make it a versatile ingredient for a sacred sanctuary, depending on the nature of your intention:

- *Texture:* Is it rough, smooth, soft, shiny, or ridged? Is it thick or thin?
- *Color:* Is it pale or vibrant? Is it fiery or cool?
- *Imagery:* Does it evoke a specific place or time? Tell a story?
- *Function*: Where will you place it and for what purpose? Will your fabric be a rug, a curtain, an altar cloth, or a wall hanging?

Religious Figurines, Icons, and Relics

Religious figurines and icons that represent divine figures within your own religion, philosophy, or cultural background can be used to deepen your connection to a living tradition. Their images bring wisdom, comfort, and guidance into your sacred space. It is a way to honor them and form an intimate relationship, so that their gifts become more available to you as you learn to embody your personal faith. You may also borrow deities from world wisdom traditions that speak to your soul—even going back to antiquity.

Consider placing representations on your altar or in your shrine of:

- goddesses and gods.
- angels.
- saints.
- spiritual teachers.
- prophets and sages.

Figurines are generally small enough to place on an altar, and therefore many people will use more than one. However, if you are devoting an entire shrine to a particular divinity, you may prefer to obtain a larger sculpture. Icons are usually paintings hung on the wall above an altar or shrine, or set upon it. Relics are objects that have actually been touched or worn as clothing by a saint or spiritual master. These items are much more rare ingredients to possess, and often fragile, so they would usually be kept in a box or framed under glass for protection. When they are available, you may also use photographs of spiritual teachers and modern saints for sacred ingredients.

Hindu Gods and Goddesses

Hinduism is both an ancient and a living religion, which originated in India and is currently practiced by millions of people. It has a complex cosmology in which thousands of local gods and goddesses are associated with different aspects of human life, and the divine masculine and divine feminine are equally honored. In the West, we have begun to assimilate information about the spiritual paths of this religion, including *karma* or *action*, *jnana* or *knowledge*, and *bhakti* or *devotion*. As we explore Eastern meditation, yoga, and music, we also become more aware of Hindu deities. No matter what your background is, perhaps these deities can inspire you and accompany you on your sacred journey.

Here is a brief listing of major Hindu gods and goddesses; the first three represent the trinity of the endless creative and destructive cycles:

- Brahma: Creator of the universe.
- Vishnu: Sustainer of the universe.
- Shiva: Destroyer of the universe.
- Lakshmi: Goddess of prosperity, purity, chastity, and generosity.
- Parvati: Goddess of marriage (in her aspect as Kali she is symbolic of transformation and destruction).
- Krishna: God of love and the destruction of evil.
- Ganesh: God of knowledge, remover of obstacles, bringer of blessings.

Shiva as Nataraj, Lord of the Dance. His dance manifests creation, sustenance, destruction, balance, and liberation.

Ancient Egyptian Gods and Goddesses

In ancient Egypt, people believed in multiple gods and goddesses, who varied from region to region and evolved over the 4,000-year span of that civilization. The hieroglyphic writings on the walls of monumental pyramids, temples, and burial chambers tell stories about spiritual travels into the eternal afterlife. The writings are also considered "textbooks" of knowledge. The gods and goddesses were a family whose members were sovereign over different aspects of life experience in the physical plane.

In your sacred space, you can use hieroglyphics, framed papyrus paintings, and figurines of the ancient Egyptian deities as ingredients that evoke the resonance of specific qualities of being that you wish to celebrate and energize. Deities were often associated with animals and elements of nature. Here are a few:

- *Isis:* The Divine Mother, the archetypal feminine. Goddess of devotion, magical skills, motherhood, and loyalty. In hieroglyphs she wears wings and has a throne on her head.

- *Horus:* God of prophecy, humor, music, art, communication, and the balance of the natural elements. In hieroglyphs he is depicted with the head of a falcon.

- *Nephthys:* Goddess of the shadow, grief, intuition, and guardianship. She wears a house on her head, symbolic of retreat.

- *Khnum:* God of new life, language, creativity, and procreation. He is depicted with the head of a ram, and as a potter because he can turn dreams into reality.

- *Maat:* Goddess of truth, divine order, justice, the law, and integrity. She wears a feather on her head, which is weighed against the human heart after death.

- *Thoth:* God of healing, wisdom, science, and writing. He is depicted with the head of an ibis and is said to have invented hieroglyphs.

- *Sekmet:* Goddess of destruction and rebirth, and divine judgment. She is depicted with the head of a lioness and is said to eat liars.

Ancient Greek Gods and Goddesses

Like the Egyptians, the people of ancient Greece believed in a pantheon of deities who were related in various ways and oversaw aspects of life and certain qualities. Their mythology was carved into stone friezes that ran along the tops of temples. Roman deities were the counterparts of the Greek pantheon.

Some of the most influential Greek gods and goddesses include:

- *Zeus:* The Divine Father (Roman: Jupiter).
- *Hera:* The Divine Mother (Roman: Juno).
- *Poseidon:* The god of the sea (Roman: Neptune).
- *Athena:* The goddess of wisdom and science (Roman: Minerva).
- *Dionysus:* The god of ecstasy (Roman: Bacchus).
- *Artemis:* The goddess of women's autonomy and the moon (Roman: Diana).
- *Aphrodite:* The goddess of love and beauty (Roman: Venus).
- *Hermes:* The god of commerce and speed (Roman: Mercury).

Celtic and Scandinavian Gods and Goddesses

The Celtic tradition encompasses England, Ireland, Wales, Scotland, Brittany, and the Isle of Man, so it contains a wide variety of legends and lore. It was the prominent pre-Christian belief system in these regions, and survives today most notably in the forms of Wicca, modern Paganism, and Celtic shamanism. Most of the mythology comes from fragments of text that were transcribed on vellum and parchment between the 12th and 15th centuries. Some has been passed down in stories and songs. Interestingly, although the Celtic deities are eternal, they are not immortal. Throughout the year, they die and are reborn. Their changes are profoundly linked to seasonal cycles and nature.

The Scandinavian pre-Christian tradition similarly encompasses a large region. It belongs to the Norwegian, Swedish, Danish, and Icelandic people. The mythology comes down to us from sagas and eddas, which were ultimately transcribed. They represent a multi-layered worldview that has parallels in other cosmologies. If your ancestry is in one of these cultures, you may find these ancient deities meaningful and resonant. In which case, I recommend doing some research in a library or on the Internet to figure out which god or goddess would be your best inspiration or guide for your intentions.

Angels and Archangels

St. Thomas Aquinas wrote: "Angels transcend every religion, every philosophy, every creed. In fact angels have no religion as we know it . . . their existence precedes every religious system that has ever existed on earth." Judaism, Christianity, and Islam, among other faiths, believe that angels act as intermediaries between the Divine and human beings. Angels are genderless beings of light and have no bodies, although they can assume different forms when they choose. Many people believe in guardian angels and angels are often celebrated in art. These images can sanctify your sacred space.

The only four archangels found in the Bible are Michael, Gabriel, Raphael, and Uriel, although people of different faiths believe in additional archangels. Each performs specific tasks and represents certain qualities.

- **Michael** ("Like God"): Michael is archangel of careers, courage, achievements, empowerment, and motivation. As the ultimate protector against evil, he is often depicted holding the scales of justice or a fiery sword. He represents the element of Earth and the direction North.
- **Gabriel** ("God Reveals"): Gabriel is the archangel of annunciation, revelation, truth, justice, and hope. He rules communication and brave new ideas. He represents the element of Water and the direction West.
- **Raphael** ("God Heals"): Raphael is the archangel of healing, prayer, love, joy, providence, science, and knowledge. He is the patron of healers, happy meetings, and travelers. He represents the element of Fire and the direction South.
- **Uriel** ("God is Light" or "The Fire of God"): Uriel is the archangel of ancient wisdom, universal order, magic,

astrology, salvation, judgment, enlightenment, insights, and sudden changes. He is often depicted with fire blazing in his palms, symbolizing transmutation and purification of emotions and thoughts by divine love. He represents the element of Air and the direction East.

Christian Saints

Saints are people who have lived a life dedicated to God and are recognized by the Catholic Church as holy and illustrious spiritual masters. Many of them faced unspeakable cruelty and all of them performed bona fide miracles. While some lived only a short time ago, even those who departed centuries ago are still revered today and called on for spiritual strength, support, and wisdom. When you include a saint's image in your sacred sanctuary, you can call upon them and they become spiritually available to support your request. If you would like to learn more about saints and find one that can be a patron to your special cause, then I urge you to research and learn more about these holy masters so that they can become more "real" and available to you.

Here are a few of these renowned and holy sages:

- **Saint John the Baptist:** St. John was cousin to Jesus Christ and chosen to prepare Christ's way. He was so widely acknowledged as a holy man that when he preached the coming of a messiah, he was often mistaken for him.

- **Saint Jude:** St. Jude is known as the patron saint of desperate situations. One of the 12 apostles who followed Jesus, he has been mistaken for Jesus' betrayer, Judas Iscariot. People have found solace, support, and solutions to seemingly unsolvable problems when they have invoked St. Jude to help them in their time of need.

- **Saint Bernadette:** Bernadette was a poor, sick child working as a shepherd in Lourdes, France, when the Virgin Mary appeared to her on February 11, 1858 and told her to have the priest build a chapel there. Today, many pilgrims journey to this sacred site to pray in the church and drink of the healing waters.

- **Saint Francis of Assisi:** St. Francis was born into a wealthy Italian family in the middle ages. When Christ appeared to him and told him, "Repair my falling house," he took this literally and gave away all his worldly goods to help a local priest rebuild his church. He then existed in poverty, living in caves, and communing with the birds and animals. He founded several religious orders and spent the rest of his life caring for the sick and poor. He is the patron saint of animals and ecology.

- **Saint Teresa of Avila:** Born in 1515 in Spain, St. Teresa entered a convent when she was 15. She was alternately physically ill or made ecstatic by mystical visions and experiences, thus she is known as the patron saint of migraine sufferers and people with heart disease.

Photographs, Prints, and Paintings

Hanging photographs in your sanctuary of your loved ones—spouses, life partners, children, friends, and lovers—or a hero whom you admire is a way of connecting to these individuals both emotionally and spiritually. In your office, you might honor the influence of an innovative thinker, brilliant artist, or remarkable leader, such as Albert Einstein, Georgia O'Keefe, or Nelson Mandela. Photographs bring a subject's soul essence into your space.

Are there any special places that you have been to or long to go? Especially, a sacred site, such as the pyramids of Egypt, holy temples in Tibet, the birthplace of Jesus, or the shrines of Fatima or Lourdes? Photographs can bring these alive in your home or office sanctuary as well. Maybe you took a travel snapshot that came out well. You could get it enlarged and hang it in a lovely frame to stimulate your memories of a past adventure or the people you met.

Mountains, rivers, and other awesome natural sites can make exhilarating and transcendent ingredients. Photographic prints of natural parks and wilderness areas are easy to come by. Perhaps you were born in farmland, but now live in a city. You could celebrate the essence of your childhood environment by hanging a photo of a ripening field of wheat blown by the wind. It is also possible to acquire prints of the moon and other celestial bodies—galaxies, stars, and planets—taken by astronomers.

Paintings of places and painted portraits can bring similar energy into your sanctuary that actual photographs and prints of photographs do. Some people prefer one artistic medium to the other. Paintings have added qualities, because different materials generate different textures, and they have the potential to be more abstract, however, a photograph and a painting both reflect the sensibility of their creators. The best rule of thumb is that your photographs, prints, and paintings should be meaningful, inspiring, and food for your soul.

Sacred and Mystical Symbols and Artifacts

Sacred and mystical symbols and artifacts can add energy and meaning to your altar, shrine, or sanctuary. Throughout history, people have been using symbols to understand and harness the elemental forces of the natural world, as well as supernatural or divine energy. From the earliest cave drawings to Egyptian hieroglyphs, from the Christian cross to the Star of David, symbols and artifacts have been used to relate to the mysterious forces around us from the very beginning. In many ancient cultures, using sacred symbols in a home was considered essential to ensure the well-being of its inhabitants. Though specific symbols have changed through the ages, according to the dictates of culture and fashion, some have remained in constant use, despite the shifting winds of time. These symbols have a power of their own. Not only does the shape of an individual symbol affect the flow of energy in its surroundings, the hundreds of years of use also strengthen its intangible power and resonance.

It is fascinating that many sacred and mystical symbols represent the fundamental qualities of physical phenomena. For example, a circle can be used to illustrate the cycles of days, seasons, phases of the moon, and planets in our solar system. It also signifies union and equality, because it is perfectly contained and balanced.

The symbol "Om"

In rituals, a circle can also become a power tool when it becomes the shape of a consecrated space or when celebrants walk, dance, or otherwise move along its circumference.

Sacred and mystical symbols and artifacts usually work on multiple levels at the same time. Their different meanings connect us to nature, history, and tradition. Some incorporate numbers, such as the seven candles in a menorah, which embody the seven days of creation and the seven archangels, but at the same time remind us of the story of Hanukah and Jewish tradition. Others contain letters or words, believed to contain the power of thought, intention, and universal sounds. The way they have been used in traditional religious practices or by your own family also contributes to their resonance.

The following is a list of sacred and mystical symbols and artifacts, along with some of their meanings and cultural contexts. Remember that the meanings for symbols can vary from culture to culture and through different historical periods. In your home sanctuary, there are many ways to incorporate them into an altar or shrine, and use them as decorations. Many of these kinds of ingredients are also frequently used as power tools. In a certain respect, you are only limited by the extent of your imagination. For example, a cross may be sewn into the fabric of an altar cloth or mounted on the wall, several objects laid flat on an altar can also form this shape, and the shape itself can be used as a gesture, or a cross may be used as a power tool to accomplish a purpose within a ceremony.

As with other ingredients, I recommend that you choose those for your sanctuary that speak to your heart and pertain to your intentions.

- *Ankh:* An ancient Egyptian cross that represents eternal life and sexual union. It incorporates both male and female principles in the shapes of circle and rod.
- *Bowl:* Like cups and cauldrons, bowls are female objects that represent the womb and the Cosmic Mother. As a power tool, bowls can be used to mix or contain substances, and, if they are made of metal or stone, for burning herbs and incense.
- *Circle:* This is one of the most potent symbols. It represents eternity, completion, unity, the universe, wholeness, equality, and perfection. It also signifies the Divine feminine. All of Native American culture revolved

around the circle. This was because their concept of life was circular rather than linear. The great round sun rises and sets in an enormous circle, as does the moon. The planets and universe move in a circular, gravitational pull.

- *Cross:* This symbol predates Christianity and symbolizes eternal life, resurrection, and divine protection. In Christianity, it represents Jesus Christ, Christ's death by crucifixion and his resurrection. It also represents the enlightenment and salvation he brought to the world.

- *Cup:* This symbol represents the female principle. It recalls the Holy Grail, the legendary cup from which Christ drank at the Last Supper, as well as the Celtic cauldron of generation. Cups are used as power tools in rituals for pouring libations and sharing sips of beverages. The cauldron, like the cup, is a female symbol, representing both the womb and also the oceans.

- *Dreamcatcher:* A protective power tool hung above the bed to entrap the energy of dreams, as a spider snares flies in a web.

- *Eye of Horus:* From ancient Egypt, a hieroglyphic eye that represents expanded awareness and clairvoyance, or specifically the moment of "third eye" awakening.

- *Infinity sign:* This symbol represents endless continuity and limitlessness. It looks like a number eight lying on its side. Originally drawn as two circles touching, it embodies both the male and female principles. Now it is used mathematically to signify numbers or series too great to be measured or counted.

A Native American dreamcatcher

- *Menorah:* A candelabrum, lit ceremonially by members of the Jewish faith during the celebration of Hanukah.

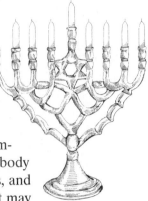

- *Mezuzah:* Many Jewish people hang small metal boxes called mezuzahs on their doorframes for protection, which are rubbed on entering. These contain specific written passages from the Torah.

- *Pentacle:* A five-pointed star that symbolizes life, health, and the human body (the points represent the head, hands, and feet). With the single point upright, it may be used for protection.

- *Pyramid:* In the ancient Mayan and Aztec cultures, sacred temples were housed in flat-topped pyramids that incorporated astronomical calendars in their architectural design. The ancient Egyptians also built elaborate sacred pyramids as tombs for the pharaohs and entrances to the after-life. A four-sided pyramid is an inherently strong structure and regarded by many people to have special energetic properties.

- *Runes:* An ancient Nordic-Germanic alphabet of mystical letters that are used for divining. There are no curved lines or circles. They are usually carved into small stones or wooden blocks.

- *Star of David:* In Judaism, a symbol of good luck, also known as the "Shield of David." A hexagram composed of two equilateral triangles superimposed.

- *Triangle:* The triangle embodies the power of the pyramids. It relates to the combined power of the body, mind, spirit in each person; the past, present, future; the Father, Son, and Holy Spirit of the Christian Trinity; the Triple Goddess of antiquity—the Maiden, Matron, and Crone; and a family unit of father, mother, and child.

- *Trigrams:* Eight figures from the Chinese I Ching, *The Book of Changes*, composed of sets of broken and complete lines. They combine four elements with four sub-elements and correspond to the compass directions and aspects of human experience. Each feng shui bagua zone is associated with a specific trigram.

* *Zodiac signs:* Twelve astrological symbols pertaining to the locations of the sun, moon, and planets at different times. This system of divination probably dates back to pre-history. Many ancient Egyptian temples contain these symbols, which probably date back to the Sumerian civilization.

Talismans

Talismans are objects that bring good luck. They are often associated with superstition and folkloric beliefs. Usually they are small enough to fit in the palm of your hand, carry in a pocket, or wear on a chain around your neck. Some are culturally recognized items, such as a "lucky" rabbit's foot or a Greek eye-bead that wards off evil thoughts and ill wishes. Carvings of scarabs are used as talismans to the present day, ever since the ancient Egyptians first noticed that these golden-colored beetles resembled the sun, which they worshipped. Native Americans wear medicine pouches around their necks that may contain sacred herbs, stones, and other spiritual items.

Talismans can also be eclectic objects that only have personal meaning, such as mementoes of places you've been or people you've known. You might gather a bit of soil from the sacred sites in foreign countries you've visited and keep them in small vials, or wear a locket with a tress of hair from the head of a beloved. I have a friend who had a fascination with keys as a child. Her grandmother gave her an ornate antique key that she kept as a talisman for many years.

Being able to touch a talisman is part of its charm. There is immediacy to the power of these items. You can use them instantly to ground you in a spiritual essence or remind you of a specific intention or loving thought you wish to hold in mind. Many cultures and religious traditions understand this power to connect to a higher reality through touch. Holy medals, scapulars, and rosaries, Buddhist prayer beads, and "worry" beads can be used to focus the mind and count repetitions while performing prayers, mantras, and prostrations. Talismans of these sorts make wonderful power tools.

Beautiful, Favorite, and Natural Objects

Give your favorite and beautiful objects a place in your sacred space. The little items of meaning and beauty in our lives are treasures of the heart. These could be handicrafts, lace, mementos, and special heirlooms that have, over time, become imbued with grace, meaning, and sacredness.

Among many of the small treasures I have saved over the years are some "Holy Cards," which are like prayer cards of the Catholic faith. These small cards, approximately 2 x 4 inches, are given out during special occasions, such as to commemorate the passing of a loved one, or to commemorate important events in one's Christian life, such as at a child's first communion and other sacramental rituals. These cards usually feature a picture of Jesus, Mary, or an honored saint on one side, and a prayer invoking their support on the other side. If it is marking a special occasion, they are sometimes personalized with the name of the person being honored or remembered.

What makes my collection meaningful to me is that I have many of the cards that were given to my mother when she was young and at Catholic boarding school. These cards are delicate, dating back to the early 1930s, and come from Europe. Some are made of lace with Victorian detailing, and others are decorated in the art deco style of the time. Some are simple and childlike, and others are intricate and ornate. They are special heirlooms invisibly suffused over the years by the subtle intentions of my mother's prayers.

Natural objects possess the chi of the environment they come from, and can imbue you with a sense of what is timeless and important. You can activate the energy of an altar or shrine by choosing inanimate, yet meaningful, items from nature, such as leaves, seashells, pinecones, feathers, birds' nests, and rocks. These treasures serve as visual reminders of the natural world. My friend JoAnn, for instance, collects pebbles shaped like hearts. She lives in a beach community, and whenever she takes a walk along the shore, she keeps her eyes out for these little treasures. She has several on her desk and several more on a table by her front door.

Some people place bundles of dried herbs on their altars. Use herbs that correlate with your intentions, such as lavender for relaxation and healing, or sage for cleansing and purifying. If you find colorful autumn leaves while you are out walking, place them on your altar for inspiration. These symbolize the seasons and cycles of nature. Each kind of tree has its own special essence. Correlate the leaves or seeds you include with the intention you have set for your shrine. For instance, pinecones represent fertility. Maple leaves represent growth and prosperity.

Seashells are often a resonant symbol, especially if you have hand-picked them along the shore. As a young adult, I traveled extensively and collected shells from many remote and exotic locales around the globe. I consider my collection of shells a special treasure. Because shells evoke the power of the sea and the primal essence of life emerging from the water, they are often used to decorate altars and shrines.

A stone referred to as the omphalos has been traditionally used to symbolize the "power center" of a village or a sacred site. This symbolic stone is believed to anchor concentrated energy from the earth. Lingams are a type of stone found in the Narmada River in India, where the river currents have tumbled them into their characteristic oval shape. They are well known for harnessing and grounding energy in sacred spaces, particularly in gardens, and for emitting powerful energy fields. In the temples of India and Tibet, they are reverently cared for and honored. At the home sanctuary of my friend, Tara, two lingams rest upright near the front door to her yoga studio.

Crystals and Gemstones

Crystals and gemstones are abundant, colorful, and fascinating. An eighth of the world's crust is quartz crystal, for instance. Like plants and animals, minerals are attuned to universal life force energy. They are known for their piezoelectric properties. The many varieties resonate with different qualities of being, and therefore can help you to align with your intentions in different areas of your life. This makes them excellent ingredients and power tools for a home sanctuary, altar, or shrine.

Choosing Your Crystal or Gemstone

When you are shopping for a crystal or gemstone, be sure to pick them up. If you are sensitive to the movement of energy, you may notice a slight prickling, tingling, or pulsing in your hands that emanates from the crystals and stones. That's the piezoelectric force mentioned previously. Each kind of crystal has a special energy signature and even two stones of the same type often have very different essences. Handling it is a way of sensing whether an energy essence is resonant with yours. If you cannot actually feel the currents, simply trust and allow your intuition to guide you.

Every crystal and gemstone has a color, a shape, and an energy that may be appropriate for your purposes. Here are a few types:

- **Amethyst:** calms, increases spiritual awareness, and removes negativity.
- **Aquamarine:** soothes emotions, inspires compassion and tranquility.
- **Bloodstone:** creates health, mental balance, courage, and success.
- **Carnelian:** removes fears, creates enthusiasm, concentration, and goodwill.
- **Citrine:** creates health, transmutes fear, and opens the mind.
- **Garnet:** brings health, emotional balance, and prosperity.
- **Hematite:** grounds and calms.
- **Jade:** supports wisdom, blessings, clarity, and is soothing.
- **Lapis lazuli:** grounding yet spiritual, supports wisdom, love, creativity, and expression.
- **Malachite:** good for babies, aids sleeping, promotes inner security, insight, and protects against mishaps.
- **Moonstone:** good for motherhood, night travel, consciousness, and reconciliation.
- **Onyx:** promotes stability, balance, letting go, separation, and transformation of the shadow self.
- **Quartz:** supports purification, protection, and spiritual awakening.
- **Rose quartz:** promotes love, romance, and friendship.
- **Sapphire:** helps enlightenment, divinity, peace, and devotion.

- **Tiger's eye:** enhances clairvoyance and improves discernment.
- **Topaz:** restores energy, uplifts, enhances friendship and love.
- **Tourmaline:** supports optimism, understanding, inspiration, and perseverance.

Clearing Your Crystal or Gemstone

Once you have brought your crystal or gemstone home, it is important to do an energy clearing on it to remove the energy impurities of others who may previously have handled it. Repeat the process every so often as your crystal gathers new energy and impurities in your sacred space. There are many methods of cleansing. Deliberately set the intention of purification and then:

- *Water:* Hold the stone under running water or place it in a fresh flowing stream. **Note:** Some stones disintegrate in water!
- *Ice:* Place the stone or crystal in a freezer overnight. **Note:** Thawing may disintegrate some stones (as above for water purification)!
- *Sunlight/Moonlight:* Place the stone in a sunny spot or where the moon will shine upon it for several hours. **Note:** Some crystals lose color in direct light!
- *Earth:* Bury your crystal overnight in the soil.
- *Salt:* Bury your crystal in a bowl of rock salt for a couple of days.

Once you have cleansed your crystal and prior to placing it in your sanctuary or on your altar, spend time meditating to welcome it and endow it with your intention. Respectfully ask that it serve this sacred purpose. Express your gratitude.

Animal Totems

An animal totem, such as a mammal or a bird, or even a mythological creature, can serve as a distinctive, and often venerated, symbol of spiritual guidance. The belief in totem spirits and guardians can be found throughout the world and in every historical era. They are frequently considered the emblem or protector of an entire family, group, or clan, such as those seen on coats of arms and heraldic banners in medieval Europe. Native Americans give credence to the protective spirit of an animal ally or protector, as do Shamans and indigenous cultures from other regions of the world.

You can bring the powerful energy of a totem into your sanctuary in the form of a statue, carving, painting, photograph, or other representation. You can add a feather, horn, or shell that has come into your possession after being cast off by your totem creature. Whatever the form, an object that honors a totem can bestow the qualities of that animal—an important element to making an altar or sacred space a safe haven. It is a means of drawing the guardian spirit to create a protective energy around your sanctuary. It is also a way to focus your intention to embody an essence, or quality that a totem possesses, such as the playfulness of a dolphin or the courage of a lion. Usually an intention is made stronger if it pertains to the purpose of the altar or sacred space as well as to the individual who placed the totem object.

Call forth the totem energy that suits your specific purpose. For instance, if you are making an altar for someone who is sick, you may want to call forth the healing energy of the bear. Totem characteristics associated with the energy of the bear include: healing, protection of the young, strength, and helpfulness in working with dreams. If you are making an altar to enhance prosperity and abundance in your life, you may want to call forth the powerful energy of the buffalo. Characteristics associated with the buffalo include: prosperity, power, steady progress, and strength.

You can discover your personal totem or guardian animal in several ways: through an experience, in a dream, or by an intuitive exercise. Finding a totem usually involves an inner journey. Notice different animals, birds, fish, or reptiles that are attracting your attention. Observe how they look, sound, and behave. Do you have any emotional attraction to the animal, feelings such as awe, admiration, respect, humor, affection, empathy, or fear? Do you attribute any specific qualities or associations to the creatures? What are your cultural beliefs about their powers? Through this process, your animal ally will begin to reveal itself. Trust your inner voice. Connecting with your totem may not be a linear process of discovery and inquiry. It is a cumulative experience of developing clarity.

Your power animal may simply have been your favorite animal since childhood, or it may be an animal that you are inexplicably drawn to at this time of your life. Most often, you will share qualities and characteristics with your totem. Totems can change over time, as you pass from one stage of life to another. Once you have determined your totem, place physical representations of it in your sanctuary, on your altar, and around your home. Invoke, or call upon it consciously for assistance and guidance. Remember to express your respect and gratitude when you do.

The following are the meanings and metaphysical attributes of various totems:

- **Bear:** wisdom, healing, dream keeping, and protective mothering.
- **Butterfly:** spiritual enlightenment.
- **Cat:** intuition, independence, and alertness.
- **Coyote:** growth, transformation, and irony.
- **Crane:** birth, longevity, and endurance.
- **Cricket:** household luck.
- **Dog:** companionship, loyalty, and protection.
- **Dolphin:** psychic telepathy, intelligence, individual freedom coupled with group cooperation, and playfulness.
- **Eagle:** leadership, strength, and higher spirit.
- **Elephant:** wisdom, memory, and community.
- **Frog:** transformation and magic.
- **Hawk:** messenger, business acumen, and independence.
- **Horse:** empathy, strength, travel, and vision.
- **Hummingbird:** speed and brilliance.
- **Lion:** courage, nobility, and protection.
- **Owl:** prophecy, wisdom, and vision.
- **Rabbit:** alertness, fertility, mischief, and good luck.
- **Seahorse:** tranquility.
- **Snake:** healing and knowledge.
- **Swan:** enlightenment and beauty.
- **Tiger:** protection and leadership.

- ◆ **Turtle:** patience, stability, and longevity.
- ◆ **Whale:** knowledge, ancestral memory, and unconditional love.
- ◆ **Wolf:** community, hunting, and warrior spirit.

Inspirational Books, Cards, Poems, and Quotations

Words have always been understood to have power, as they are symbols of thoughts and intentions. Therefore, keeping spiritual books in your sacred space can provide inspiration and guidance. Use sacred reading material as a power tool or an ingredient to anchor specific resonant ideas. These could include holy books, such as the Bible, the Koran, the Bhagavad-Gita, Tao Te Ching, and the Haggadah, ecstatic love poems written by the renowned Sufi poet Rumi or other poets, or contemporary books devoted to personal empowerment.

There are many inspirational cards available today that range from the kind you might find at your local church or temple to the varieties of "over-the-counter" inspirational messages in card decks, from tarot to angel cards, from mantra cards to yoga cards, from *Conversations with God* cards (by Neale Donald Walsch) to the wisdom cards of Louise Hay, and many, many more.

You might also write your own prayers and intentions on a slip of paper and place them on or above an altar. Or have your loved ones provide you with their written notes. Personal expressions of love can deeply touch our hearts and souls. Try filling a basket with blessings and affirmations that you can reach into and select from. Or purchase a small deck of angel cards that you can draw from before a meditation as guidance. On a desktop, you can post a quotation in a particular bagua zone to amplify its energy.

Art Supplies and Writing Materials

It is a good idea to keep a journal, pens, and art supplies available in your sacred space to write, draw, or otherwise make art. Making these power tools available gives you an opportunity to access your creativity and lets your subconscious mind express itself. You may only write in your journal occasionally, but sometimes it is helpful to create treasure maps and wish lists.

For inspiration and to allow your subconscious mind to "speak" to your conscious mind, try the following activity:

CREATING A TREASURE MAP

A treasure map is an artistic vision of your ideal life, a collage board upon which you paste images and words cut out from magazines and newspapers to create scenes, and add your own drawings. Like an affirmation, you will embellish your treasure map with positive statements in the present tense, so your mind believes it's all happening now.

Here's an example of how you might make a treasure map if your intention were to create a relationship:

First, you would take a 12" x 14" piece of cardboard and start collecting materials, such as Valentine's Day magazine advertisements picturing a couple at a spa and words like "romance," "intimacy," and "love," or phrases like, "I cherish you" and "being available." Ground these in the present with "I am" or "Now."

Then, once you've collected every element you desire and need for your vision of an ideal relationship, create a visual scene, or map of the relationship by pasting your ingredients on your collage board. Design your treasure map in a feng shui way, by using the *bagua* to help you determine your layout.

Instruments

Some of the most potent power tools are instruments. They can also offer us great pleasure and emotional release. As you saw in Chapter 3, sound is an energy enhancer because it tangibly stimulates the ambient chi in any space. This is also why it is often used in space clearing rituals (Chapter 2). Instruments create sound, but they may also be used as decorative ingredients. They are often significant mementos of foreign travels or are the tools of your own music making.

Instruments take many forms. Among others, they include drums, pipes, harps, horns, bells, and rattles. During shamanic ceremonies, drumming is frequently used to induce a trance. Some cultures use dancing to achieve states of ecstatic reverie and spiritual connection and drums provide a rhythm for the movement. Other times during rituals, instruments are harnessed to punctuate moments of intensity, when heightening of spiritual energy is required. Then the participants generate as much sound as possible, by using whatever kinds of instruments are available.

Bells and tingshaws, which we discussed in Chapter 2, are often used to open and close a sacred ceremony or ritual. Their ringing can redirect patterns of vibration and energy. Another method of heightening the energy of a shrine or sacred space is to use gongs and singing bowls. A hand-hammered gong that has been used in a temple will be imbued with the strongest and most auspicious chi. If you can procure one of these, you will have found a treasure indeed!

You can now procure quartz crystal singing bowls that resonate in different keys, which are said to open up blockages in the body's various energy centers. The vibrations of these can be very powerful, taking you deeply into your soul self. You can use them at an altar or shrine to disperse negative energy and invoke positive energy.

A Final Thought

In the following chapters, you will be learning about the art of *shrine-* and *altar-crafting* for different intentions and in different environments around your home—in its communal, intimate, creative, and contemplative areas. By then, you'll have focused on an intention, found a location, prepared the area, selected energy enhancements to balance and activate the space, and gathered your desired objects. In the process, you'll discover that the actual building of your shrine is a sacred journey, much like a ritual.

Begin by imagining again what you will do in this sacred space. Will you meditate or pray? Will you compose music or write? What symbolic objects do you require? You are about to design a unique sacred space that will reflect (to you) a vision of your inner self. It is therefore important to allow yourself freedom of creative expression.

Then, once you have gathered objects that resonate with your intentions, assemble and bless them. I usually begin with the foundation and work my way upward and circularly through the bagua zones. If you have chosen an altar cloth, drape the fabric over a flat surface to create a consecrated space. Pick colors, textures, and patterns that symbolize or correlate to your intention.

Next, place your objects on your altar. If it will help energize your intention, you may want to do so according to the zones of the bagua. Begin with a few well-chosen objects that are meaningful to you or symbolize your intention. Close your eyes and tune-in to your intuition and wisdom guides. Ask for assistance.

Let your altar grow as you add to it. Taller items should be placed towards the back of the altar with smaller objects arranged closer. This way you can easily view your treasured artifacts and objects. There is no right or wrong, just please your own intuitive sense of layout, staying mindful of your intention and praying or contemplating on your desire as you proceed.

The symbols, artifacts, and objects you choose for your home sanctuaries will help to reinforce your intentions. Thus they should reflect you and your dreams. It is not necessary that you fully comprehend the reasons why you are drawn to or resonate with a particular object or symbol. Just allow yourself to trust your inner wisdom and go with the way they make you feel. Shrine and altar tokens are valuable for the feelings and subtle energies they evoke whether they are commonplace or exotic. Even an ordinary item can be a sacred souvenir when it is displayed, as it evokes memory and reverence.

Remember, the process of altar building doesn't have to happen in a day, although some altars are created to honor specific occasions, such as a birth, marriage, or holiday. Most home altars and shrines grow over time with use and attention. They seem to have a life cycle that reflects their creators' personal evolutions, whims, and needs. Practice applying your understanding of the bagua zones, and keep in mind how important it is to create balanced energy in sacred space. Later on, in Chapter 9, we'll talk about rituals that can help activate and strengthen the energy you are setting into motion.

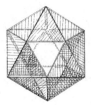

Chapter 5

Communal Rooms

"*Every life needs its altar.*
It may be in the church or a quiet nook.
It may be a moment in the day, or a mood of the heart."
—*Ester B. York*

Arranged on a cocktail table in Sam and Krista's living room, in an upscale home located in a suburb of Portland, Oregon, are what appears to be a random assortment of Krista's spiritual power tools and ingredients. Once a month, the couple invites 10 friends over for a spiritual salon. The tabletop contains crystal balls, vases of flowers, and bowls of fruit, tingshaws, bells, an incense holder, and scented wax aromatherapy beads. I have been a guest on many occasions.

Krista begins the monthly ritual by serving herbal tea while the participants quietly share small talk. Soft music plays in the background and the candles on the table provide the only light. Soon the group settles into comfortable chairs around the table. Krista lights a small amount of sage in an abalone shell and uses it to cleanse the energy of each person, smudging them with a feather beautifully decorated with ribbons and beads. She then facilitates a group discussion on a spiritual theme, such as world peace, healing, relationships, making a contribution, or raising children. A specific intention is formed from this discussion, such as "Let my friends and family be whole and happy," or "May wars and political turbulence cease and the people of all nations thrive."

Next, Sam and Krista light incense, and the group begins meditation (lasting 15 to 20 minutes) focusing on the intention. At the end, Krista or Sam softly rings the bell or tingshaw to bring everyone's attention back to the room. The discussion is resumed, during which people share their meditation experience and any insights they have gleaned. Finally, Sam recites a prayer to close the salon. He always makes it up on the spur of the moment, relating it to the evening's meditation and ensuing conversation.

Sam and Krista's tabletop altar

Communal rooms include living rooms, family rooms, kitchens, and dining areas. These are spaces designed for spending time with others, communicating and otherwise nurturing our relationships, whether on special social occasions, such as Sam and Krista's spiritual salon, or through the course of daily living. In this chapter, we'll explore ways to honor, celebrate, and enhance the sacred essence of these activities.

Remember, when you are setting intentions throughout your home and examining the purpose of different rooms, it is important to look beyond the obvious to any deeper symbolism. So ask yourself what you consider sacred about a room that is used as a gathering place for communion with your family and friends. There can be no right or wrong answer to the question; however, feng shui offers clues about certain patterns of energy that you may find useful to keep in mind.

Let's take a look now at each kind of communal room in turn.

Sacred Living Rooms and Family Rooms

Living rooms and family rooms energetically govern the kind of people you attract. How you handle the placement of furnishings, objects, and decorations in these areas influences several important aspects of your life, including your friendships and family dynamics, as well as your professional success and financial prosperity. As sacred space, these rooms must be inviting. Seating arrangements should always create a sense of security, community, and comfort both for guests and for family. An uninviting living room or family room can result in a lack of family intimacy and community. If this is an issue in your home, you may notice that you don't have friends over much.

A living room or family room is an ideal place to display your personal treasures. You must always be mindful of the energy of any object you bring into your home—especially previously owned items, such as art and antiques—because you are bringing that energy *into* your space. So choose with care. The history of all objects, including spiritual artifacts, should be carefully checked to be sure there isn't negative energy attached to them. Avoid anything from a yard sale or flea market if the owners have experienced severe misfortune such as death, divorce, or bankruptcy. Also, consider the original purpose of an antique. I avoid masks, for instance, that are associated with war, evil, or death. In addition, it is a good idea to smudge an artifact that comes from a tomb, pyramid, or temple in order to purify it.

One of the most harmonious living rooms I have ever visited belongs to J. J. and Jonathan. Their home reminds me of a Frank Lloyd Wright design because it contains a lot of stone and huge windows. Upon entering, you step into a magical wonderland of large natural boulders, trickling water fountains, and indoor trees and plants. The yin and yang energy of the room have been balanced by combining hard stone floors with soft, curving indigo colored couches. An entire flagstone wall behind their fireplace is filled with nooks and alcoves that hold candles, crystals, cultural artifacts, and spiritual figurines. At night, with the candles and fireplace aglow, it is an enchanted environment. Jonathan and J. J. are deeply connected to their community. They frequently open their home to spiritual groups for workshops and lectures. Before each event, they cleanse the space by ringing bells and Tibetan singing bowls, light incense, and say a blessing.

Because these communal areas are usually near the front door, in feng shui they are considered "front" rooms. Thus their purpose and symbolism is to put your "best foot forward" to welcome and please others and enjoy harmonious relationships. Among other things, it is where you receive guests. If the *entrance* to your home is its "mouth of chi," then think of your living room as the "face" of your house, smiling and inviting. It is important to make a good impression in a front room.

In a psychological sense, the living room is a symbol of a family's status and identity. Good feng shui in your living room, and the positive energy it holds and conveys, can enhance your reputation, business success, and financial prosperity. Consider all the time and money most of us spend on our personal appearance. Psychologically, we do the same thing with our living rooms, but instead of *hairstyles* and *makeup*, we use our *possessions* to communicate a subliminal message. What kind of energy is your living room emitting?

J. J. and Jonathan's sacred living room

Building Shrines and Altars in Your Living Room

To build an altar or shrine in your living room or family room, put into practice what you have learned already. First, do you have a specific intention? Perhaps your goal is to build stronger family relationships. Or your intention could be to enhance your friendships, or to enjoy a better business network. Another might be to initiate a romance and the creation of a family. Once you are clear about your goals, your next step is to identify a location in the room for your shrine.

Let's suppose that you want to honor your family. An ideal placement would be the bagua zone called Family and Health. To honor

Feng Shui Do's and Don'ts for Your Living Room

* **Do** place something purple in the Prosperity and Abundance corner of the living room to activate the energy of wealth.
* **Do** ensure that the main seating area is located in such a way that people can see the door. This provides comfort and security.
* **Don't** let positive energy escape the room through a fireplace. Always keep wood in it or place a decorative fireplace screen in front of it.
* **Don't** decorate with dried plants or sticks. Use living plants or—if you lack sunlight—quality silk or fabric flowers, shrubs, and plants.
* **Don't** display "dark art," such as frightening or moody paintings or photographs, as these create a negative energy field. Replace such pieces with uplifting and harmonious ones.
* **Do** check to see if the five elements are in balance.

friendships, the perfect zone would be Helpful Friends and Travel. For romance, create an altar in the zone of Marriage and Relationships. Or, if you want to improve your interactions with colleagues at work, focus on the zone of Prosperity and Abundance. Keep in mind how public or private you want your shrine or altar to be; an altar top can be quite revealing and personal. The matter is entirely up to you, but in communal rooms there may not be as much privacy as there is elsewhere in your home, such as in your bedroom.

My friends Sarah and Ethan chose their baby grand piano as the foundation of an ancestral shrine. They cleansed the energy of the living room with the sound of bells and lit a favorite incense to purify and sanctify the piano top. Afterwards, they laid a rich green velvet shawl with beaded fringe upon it to enhance the ambient energy, as green is the color associated with the feng shui zone of Family and Health.

Then they casually, but lovingly arranged beautifully framed photographs of generations of family members and special mementos on the shawl. The centerpiece was a silver candelabrum filled with long, white tapered candles, which was an heirloom from Sarah's great-grandparents.

A non-spiritual ancestral shrine

Step-by-step, Sarah and Ethan made the process of building their shrine a ritual. While lighting the candelabrum and arranging the ingredients, they reminisced and shared stories about their forbearers with their children, thus activating the shrine and imbuing it with the loving energy of their family legacy for their descendants. Their children were delighted and added their own photographs a few months later as an anniversary gift.

◆ ◆ ◆

Even if you live in a small studio apartment, you can still create an altar or shrine, as they do not need to take up much space. Use the bagua as your guide for where to locate your furniture and consider that placement sacred. Let's say you want to create an altar to attract romance. Would there be room to place a table in the Marriage and Relationship zone in your studio? You could build an altar on top of it. Or could you put your bed there (as that would be ideal)? If so, be sure to place two small and similarly sized bedside tables on either side of it. On romance altars, always remember to incorporate paired items, such as two candlesticks holding pink candles, two heart pillows, two flowers in a vase, or a figurine, photograph, or picture portraying a romantic couple.

If your bed or a table cannot fit in the zone of Marriage and Relationships, maybe there is a windowsill in this area that you can use. Find a pretty piece of fabric, perhaps lace, and place it on the sill. Arrange photos, romantic symbols, a love poem, affirmations, a silver bell, and a small pink candle in this spot. When you focus on this altar, light the candle, ring the bells, and read your poem and affirmations with fervent mindfulness.

Go back to the energy enhancements, power tools, and ingredients in Chapters 3 and 4 to see if there are some additional ways to energize your living room sanctuary. Remember to engage your senses; try music, color, *and* light!

Sacred Kitchens

The kitchen is often considered the heart of the home. Energetically it governs abundance and well-being, since it is where we are nourished both physically and emotionally. In feng shui, food preparation is considered part of the process of sustaining our life force and bodies. It is also an extension of the exchange of giving and receiving between people. Many people believe that cooking is a holy activity, analogous to delivering an offering of love—and making the kitchen a sort of temple. In contemporary homes, the kitchen is also the room in which recycling usually occurs; it is a space that not only contributes to our own health, but also a sacred space to honor and contribute to the healing and wholeness of the planet.

Your kitchen has your soul's signature imprinted on it through near constant use. Consider the amount of time you spend there every day. Perhaps you share breakfast with your mate, do homework with your kids, or sip coffee and chat with friends who've dropped by for impromptu visits. People spontaneously gather in kitchens during parties, and in many homes it is the most communal area. Witness the shift in architectural design in the last 10 to 15 years that supports the trend of the home-based lifestyle. Today, kitchens are often large, open arenas that combine space for meal preparation and eating, as well as entertaining and a broad variety of family activities. They are spaces to establish healthy patterns of relationship that will resonate throughout your life.

Whether or not you do a lot of cooking, it is important to create an inviting and nurturing cooking space. The energy of your kitchen should be free flowing. Be sure that this area is light and bright, clean, and clutter free. Frequent space clearing is a must; every week or two, swiftly clear the ambient energy by clapping or ringing bells.

Building Shrines and Altars in Your Kitchen

You may already have a shrine in your kitchen and not realize it! This could be a refrigerator door used to display children's artwork, candid

photographs, greeting cards, and reminders of events. Or it could be a windowsill that's holding treasured tokens, spiritual icons, and objects of sensual beauty like candles, flowers, and incense. Can you see yet that an altar doesn't have to be complicated? Some people hang cork message boards in their kitchens on which they tack inspiring quotes, favorite cartoons, and personal affirmations in addition to their weekly schedules. If you place a shrine like this near your back door, whenever you go in and out of the house you will be reminded of who you really are, your soul's calling, and what matters most to you.

Altars need to be tended in order to keep their energy flowing, which makes the kitchen an ideal spot for an altar. You are likely to see it there every day and at the very least give it a brief mental acknowledgment. Better still: keep energy moving by placing new objects there, such as fresh fruit and flowers, or lighting a candle. Also rearrange it from time to time, so it remains meaningful. By tending to an altar, you are symbolically nurturing the sacred within yourself, your family, and your world.

Feng Shui Do's and Don'ts for Kitchens

- **Do** keep the burners on your stove in good working order, as their Fire energy represents your wealth.
- **Don't** locate the stove and sink directly next to each other, as Water energy douses fire. However, conveniently place them near enough to avoid spills.
- **Do** ensure that you can see the doorway when you are cooking at the stove. If the door is behind you, hang a mirror above the stove.
- **Don't** buy or rent a home where the front door enters directly into the kitchen. If you do, the people in your household may experience weight problems.

A Family Affair

Well-organized and bubbly, Paula loved taking care of her three kids. She and her husband Mark were fortunate that she could be a stay-at-home mom and dedicate herself to raising them. Over time, she had become the quintessential "soccer mom" and found herself driving from one end of town to the other, taking the children to their practices and games after school and on weekends. By the time everyone got home, there would still be dinner to prepare and homework to check afterwards. Even though Mark wanted to help out, he often got home late from his job as a salesman in a technology firm.

It seemed as though Paula's family lived in the kitchen. Between fixing breakfast, lunch, and dinner, doing dishes, laundry, and homework, and talking on the phone, the kitchen was the central hub of their home. On the outside, Paula looked like she was handling it pretty well, but on the inside, she was crumbling. She felt increasingly irritable and exhausted. When she decided it was time to make some changes, she reached out to me for advice. We talked and found that she loved her active lifestyle, but never felt centered. There seemed to be no time to stop and become present to the moment—the "Now."

During our consultation, Paula's heartfelt intention became clearer. In the midst of all the action, she wanted to connect to her deeper self, to find a way of going inward, even if only for a holy instant. She also wanted her family to access this possibility for themselves. We identified the kitchen breakfast table as a place to carve out an altar. Its purpose would be to anchor her spiritual energy and help her to go within, reflect, and regain her center and bring the family together more. When she polled her family for their approval, everyone was excited and agreed to participate. Her kids thought the whole idea was pretty cool—especially since she invited them to have a role in creating it!

Paula and Mark decided to make a game out of the whole process. After dinner one evening, they held a small ceremony, with cake and ice cream, to inaugurate the building of the altar space. They washed down the table and used bells, toy drums, and the kids' other musical instruments to cleanse the ambient energy. Then, as a group, the family chose a pretty, round tablecloth as their altar cloth. It was everyone's favorite even though it had a few stains. When Paula and Mark decided it was time for the kids to go to bed, they reinforced the purpose of the altar by suggesting that every day, for the next three days, each family member would place a meaningful possession on it. That night, the kids went to sleep imagining and dreaming about their first special gift.

The next morning, when they gathered for breakfast, everyone contributed an ingredient to the altar. Mark's was a candle from his den. Paula's was a small book of mealtime graces. Samantha brought her softball cap, Justin brought a toy robot, and Taylor brought his favorite stuffed animal, a little dinosaur. Then, Mark lit the candle, Paula read one of the graces from her book, and the kids explained why they had chosen their particular objects. By the time everyone went out the door, Paula felt that they had shared a very close time as a family.

You could probably call this a non-spiritual altar, but Paula found it spiritual. Each time she took a moment to rest her eyes on the objects and thought about the sweet story of why they had been chosen, *she found herself quietly calming and centering. Every day, she began to carve out 15 minutes to sit down at the table, light a candle, and meditate. In this way, the altar thoroughly served her intention.*

Sacred Dining Rooms

The dining room is the sacred sanctuary where we "break bread" with family and friends. The world's great religions and wisdom traditions teach us that food is a blessing from the Divine, and many people would never consider starting a meal without saying a prayer or a grace to express their gratitude for nourishment, health, abundance, and companionship. Rightly so, because thoughtfully prepared and beautifully presented meals are sacred offerings to our family and friends on the "altar" of the dinner table.

Because the dining room is intimately connected with food and the sharing of meals, it should be a space that feels emotionally nourishing. It is a uniquely auspicious place to locate an altar coordinated with holidays, celebrations, and the changing seasons. The room should be kept clean at all times and appear visually appetizing. So use furniture with beautiful linens and lovely tableware and decorations. Easy energy enhancements include different colors, flowers, candles, and music.

Planning a Ritual for Your Dining Area

Every holiday or special occasion is an opportunity to commune and share heartfelt fun and food with your loved ones. In fact, ideas on creating a sacred dining experience are so numerous that they could fill another entire book! Here are a few guidelines—always start with the basic checklist for sacred spaces:

- Is your intention a birthday party, a romantic dinner, a holiday, or a celebration? Consider decorating your dining area and creating rituals to mark the passing seasons, religious holidays, rites of passage, and life transitions, or for the purpose of family bonding, honoring friendship, and building networks.
- Your dining room table will be the location for an altar.

- Cleanse and bless the dining area with any of the methods described in Chapter 2.
- Evaluate the balance of energy in the room and select appropriate enhancements. Review the possibilities in Chapter 3.
- Drape a beautiful cloth upon the table and set out candles (Fire), flowers (Wood), dishes (Earth—unless they're *not* ceramic or porcelain), glassware (Water), and silver (Metal). The visual appeal of a lovely table by itself can create a certain mood, or theme of feelings.
- Enjoy!

Feng Shui Tips for Dining Areas

- Choose a *round* dining room table to enhance communication and comfort.
- Surround your dining table with *high-backed chairs*, as being seated with our backs exposed can cause psychological discomfort. Whenever possible, place *seats in front of solid walls*, rather than in front of windows or opening to other rooms.
- Hang a *large mirror* in your dining area, placed where it can reflect the food on the table, as this amplifies the energy of abundance.
- To secure and enhance family relationships, arrange the seating at your dining room table so that the *head of your household can see the entrance to the room*.
- Place *a bowl of fruit* on your dining table to represent "fruitful" bounty, or prosperity.

Madeleine and Stephen's Rehearsal Dinner

Madeline and Stephen were getting married, and they asked me to help them design a spiritually meaningful celebration for the rehearsal dinner. At this sacred meal, the couple intended to acknowledge their Jewish heritage and bless their coming union in the company of close family and friends. As a first step, I guided the couple through a visualization exercise with the intention of finding ideas for an occasion imbued with love. Afterwards, I facilitated them in writing down a free-flowing list of energy enhancements, ingredients, and rituals for their special evening.

We decorated the dining room together. First we blessed the space using holy water. Then we set the table for 20 people. An antique lace tablecloth, which once belonged to Madeline's grandmother, made an exquisite foundation. Upon it, we arranged a mixture of their two families' heirloom china and silver, using a pair of simple silver candelabrums to visually anchor both ends of the table. On each guest's plate, we laid an individual dinner favor: a mezuzah along with an inspirational quotation from Jewish scripture that was scripted by hand on delicate, natural, handmade paper.

The bride and groom had tested various incenses before choosing a light jasmine fragrance that would romantically fill the room with a delicate scent. When everyone sat down to dinner and the candelabrums were lit, Madeline and Stephen had everyone join hands around the table and recite in union a blessing:

"Welcome to our gathering, oh Lord.
Madeline and Stephen are beginning a great new adventure.
We acknowledge their love for you, Lord, and for each other.
We ask that You be with them on their journey.
Bless them as individuals and bless their union of love.
Be present in their daily lives, and guide them on Your path.
And, oh Lord, guide us, their friends and family, too.
So that we may support and bless their new life together."

Then each person at the table read their quotation aloud. After dessert and coffee, Madeline's close girlfriend, who is a professional singer, sang several traditional Jewish songs invoking love and God. The whole evening was a sacred celebration of love.

Communal Outdoor Spaces

In earlier times, altars and shrines were usually found in caves, niches in rock walls, groves, natural springs, or on mountaintops where people instinctively sensed the presence of the sacred. Many cultures believed that gods and goddesses lived both in the spiritual realms and also in natural, physical locations. Seekers would leave offerings and make sacrifices at these sites either to request a favor or to appease the deities. Today, we also recognize that nature is a sacred site. We understand the concept of a living, breathing planet, Gaia, imbued with spiritual energy and life. Thus gardens and outdoor terraces can make exceptional locations for communion of all kinds.

As with other areas in and around your home, to create a sacred communal garden, patio, terrace, altar, or shrine only requires one thing—your intention to make it so! Your general rule of thumb should be to *keep it simple*. Less is usually more. When planning a communal outdoor event apply these easy feng shui principles to your site:

- It should be not too hot, and not too cold.
- It should have some sunshine, and some shade.
- Combine light and bright ingredients with those that are dark and subdued.
- Combine soft shapes with hard ones.
- Combine round ingredients with angular ones.
- Make sure there is a place to sit.
- Make sure the area has a focal point, such as a pond, a view, or a statue.

Savannah's Bridal Shower

My friend Claire's niece, Savannah, had recently gotten engaged and her family was delighted. Plans were being made and an engagement party had been scheduled. Claire offered to host a bridal shower for Savannah in her home garden. Her intention was to make this shower a sacred event. When she asked for my assistance, I was thrilled!

We planned the shower for a Sunday. When the day arrived, it was gorgeous, warm, and sunny. Simply beautiful! In the morning we prepared by smudging the terrace in Claire's garden with sage and incense, and ringing bells. We had made five large posters of sacred love quotes written in a pretty Victorian script (enlarged to 3' x 5' at the local copy shop), which we now hung in various locations around the terrace, encircling the tables. The tables and chairs were white and covered with rosy pink-colored tablecloths. In the middle of each table, we set a mixed bouquet of roses in the soft colors of pink, pale yellow, rose, mauve, lavender, and ivory held in a cut glass vase, thus creating prisms of sparkling light everywhere. Each table also held a silver tray holding "angel cards," a book of affirmations, a drawstring bag of runes, and other assorted power tools.

We had been collecting rose petals from Claire's garden since the previous week, and now we had bags of them. These were scattered along a pathway that led from the driveway and around the house up to the pretty garden gate. We also sprinkled them on the tables and strew them across the stone terrace. We had filled what seemed like a billion pink-, white-, and dark rose-colored helium balloons, which we gathered into bunches and tied with pink ribbons. These were placed at the entrance to the driveway, at the garden gate, and around the perimeter of the terrace.

Best of all was the delightful ritual we had planned. In the invitations, we had instructed the guests to bring meaningful objects for a shower altar that would be created impromptu as they arrived. For its foundation, Claire and I placed a pale violet tapestry tablecloth over one of the round tables. To enhance the energy, we set a big bouquet of flowers and candles of many soft colors upon it. We also sprinkled it with rose petals.

Because this special celebration was scheduled for two days before Savannah's wedding, many of her family and friends from out of town were able to come and share it. As each woman arrived, she added her ingredient to the sacred offering.

Later, after everyone had eaten, visited, and played some of the spiritual games on the tables, we gathered around Savannah and the communal altar we had built. One by one, each guest got up, picked up her memento from the altar, and told Savannah why she choose it and why it was symbolic of her new life and her transition from "maiden" to "married woman." The objects ranged from something new to something blue to something collected at the beach. What mattered most were the poignant things that her friends and *family said to Savannah. The kind, heartfelt acknowledgments brought tears to her eyes. It was a blessed ritual.*

Of course, the day also included cake, presents, and typical aspects of a wedding shower, but I will never forget the words of love and endearment spoken by her mother and her new mother-in-law, telling Savannah how much she was cherished. It was the most unusual and heartfelt shower that any of us had attended. The day was truly sacred.

A Final Thought

Are you familiar with the saying *home is where the heart is*? Well, all sacred communal areas are "heart spaces," places to share your inner spirit and affection with those you love—your partner, family, and friends—which is why they must feel nurturing and soul-connected. Paula manifested and made room for her love to flourish through a family-built shrine. With a wedding celebration in their dining room, Madeline and Stephen embraced their friends and family and welcomed them into a circle of love. Jonathan and J. J. used their living-room fireplace to anchor their spiritual intentions in their community. Whereas for Ethan and Barbara, their ancestral shrine on the piano connected their family to the preceding generations of family. In unique ways, each one of these individuals was sharing a sacred space with those they loved.

Chapter 6

Intimate Spaces

"*An interior is the natural projection of the soul.*"
—*Coco Chanel*

he intimate spaces of your home include bedrooms, bathrooms, a home gym, and any outdoor areas where you tend to your health, rest, or pursue romance. When you explore the symbolic meaning of these rooms and sites, you will likely learn how significant to you they truly are. Your bedroom, for instance, is a sacred retreat where the soul and body can find replenishment. It is here that you can cease your activities, evade distractions, and reflect. You can cultivate solitude or enjoy quiet time in the company of your beloved or your children. In coping with the shifting demands of a busy lifestyle, a place to stabilize your energy is a necessity. The bedroom also needs to feel like a safe place in order for intimacy and relaxation to occur. It is the primary area of the home to support and celebrate your sensual nature, marriage, and togetherness.

Similarly, your bathroom is a place for self-nurturance and cleansing—personal intimacy, as well as familial intimacy. As you develop these qualities of your emotional experience, you will be able to express them more freely to others. Because a home gym is used for toning and physical exercise, its sacred purpose is the creation of health, the release of stress, and the cultivation of individual life force—although workouts may also be done in company. The sacred purpose of an outdoor spa, or an intimate gazebo in the garden would be deep relaxation and quiet sharing.

When you are setting an intention for these different rooms and sites, look beyond their surface usage and reflect upon any deeper meaning. Ask yourself what sacred purpose you want from these spaces. Explore their significance, especially in terms of intimacy, renewal, healing, and self-nurturing.

Now, let's consider each of these intimate spaces in turn.

The Spiritual Bedroom

In every moment, the universal life force is sending subtle messages to you. Listen. Everything around you is a reflection of your life and personality, including your bedroom, which is symbolic of your inner self. While your living room illustrates how you are perceived in the world, your bedroom shows how you perceive yourself deep down inside your psyche and soul. This room energetically governs the inner you.

The bedroom is an important sacred space, as it is where you spend the most time in your home. So intentions made here resonate strongly through your personal field of energy. It is used for several purposes that include sleeping, relaxing, and love making. What intention do you have in mind for this sacred space? Do you want to manifest a more active love life or to initiate a romantic relationship? Do you need more rest or to engender healing? Do you want to nurture the bonds of family? Energy enhancements and specially designed altars can assist you in anchoring these intentions.

The bedroom is an excellent place for an altar or shrine because you will see it *first*, when rising in the morning, and *last*, when going to bed at night. To your psyche these are significant moments. It is in the natural order for the body to make an organic, internal shift according to these twilight times. In the twilight of the morning, we "start our engines," so to speak. In the twilight of the evening, we slow down to rest, relax, and regroup after the day's activity.

Feng Shui Tips for Bedrooms

* Bedrooms should ideally be located in the back of the house in order to provide their inhabitants with a sense of security and comfort.

* **Do not** hang pictures of children in a master bedroom. No one wants to have children symbolically watching what's going on in the privacy of this space!

* Remove as much electronic equipment from your bedroom as you can. These devices emit electromagnetic fields that can be detrimental to your health. At the very least, unplug them while you are sleeping. Electricity is powerful Fire energy.

* Avoid having sharp-edged beams or ceiling fans located over your bed. Their chi can result in breaking up a relationship or in ill health. If they are impossible to remove, soften their presence with fabrics, or dangling crystals, and bamboo flutes.

* **Do not** place your bed in a direct line with the door, or with your feet pointing directly toward the doorway. The door is the "mouth of chi" and so the energy that enters can blast too strongly across your bed where you are vulnerable.

After you place the bagua template over the floor plan of your bedroom, aligning the "mouth of chi" with its entrance, look to see where you might locate an altar or shrine. Perhaps you have a table-top or nook? If you practice a specific religion, the bedroom can be a good place to include a prayer rug or prayer table, especially if you can carve out a niche a good distance from the bed.

Even if you do not decide to create an altar or shrine in your bedroom, there are a few important ways you can enhance the flow of energy in this special room. Doesn't it seem almost as though some rooms have a gender? Bedrooms usually have a yin—or feminine—quality to them since they are where you love, heal, and rest. Therefore, stimulate yin attributes in the bedroom. Ensure that it feels like a nest when it is time for sleeping. Think softness and roundness. Choose furnishings and materials that are relaxing and nurturing. Purchase the best quality bedding that you can afford. Choose fabrics soft and sensual to the touch. Except when necessary, keep the lighting subdued.

Women, if you want to attract a man, please keep frou frou pillows to a bare minimum . . . as well as the stuffed animal collection. Men are usually uncomfortable with all of that "girly stuff"—it's simply too much yin.

Robin's Healing Altar

Robin had survived a bout with cancer a few years prior. After surgery and some ancillary treatments, he was eventually cancer-free. Now, five years later, a different type of cancer was slowly creeping into his body. He was following his doctor's recommendations and keeping up with his treatments. Some days were good and other days he felt tired, yet he was still well enough to limit the news of his illness to his close friends and family and was able to maintain his normal schedule and activities to about the degree he had before his diagnosis. He knew the challenge was going to be tough, so he decided to place a healing altar in his bedroom and asked for my advice.

Robin's bedroom was located on the second story of his house in the bagua zone of Children and Creativity. Of course, placement in the zone of Family and Health would have been more auspicious, however, we realized that this placement could be read as a symbol of his inner child's need to feel safe and well. His wife had divorced him just after his recovery from the earlier cancer, taking the kids with her. In fact, his inner child felt abandoned and overwhelmed—not safe, not secure, and not nurtured. His emotional need was very real. I was pleased that he chose the spot he did for his healing altar. He decided to place it across from his bed, where he could easily see it when he was lying down.

Before Robin built his altar, we balanced the overall energy of the room. We cleared the space with holy water, smudging, and bells, and then he put a couple of other feng shui remedies into practice. He needed to unclutter in a major way, so he hired a professional organizer who helped him sort out and rid himself of excess belongings that were tied to the past—and that were getting in the way of a happy and healthy future. We also made sure that he got a new bed. Old beds and mattresses carry energetic imprints from their previous inhabitants. It was imperative to eliminate the imprint of Robin's marriage. I also suggested that he drape the ceiling beams over his bed with a pastel fabric to soften the impact of their "cutting chi." Sharp edges pointing toward a bed can be destructive.

Robin's altar base was an old storage trunk that was handed down through his family. He had very good familial relations, so this trunk possessed the positive energy of support and love. We neatly tucked aromatic sachets of lavender inside it to keep the linens, quilts, and blankets it held smelling sweet and clean. Over the top, he laid an heirloom tapestry. I suggested that he be conscientious about the objects that he selected as altar ingredients. They should strictly pertain to his healing process and not depart from his intention.

Robin found some pictures of himself in his happy and healthy days. He had them set into nice frames and then they went on the altar. We placed those in the Family and Health zone of the altar's bagua. He also wrote healing affirmations on cards and put them in the zone of Self-Wisdom and Knowledge. He blended the five elements of creation by using silver candlesticks (Metal), candles (Fire) in green (Wood) and yellow (Earth), flowers (Wood), and a beautiful ceramic bowl (Earth) filled with holy water (Water). Whenever he passed by or did a small ritual, he sprinkled and blessed himself with the water. Because he enjoyed the outdoors so much, his altar also held natural objects that he collected on hikes in the mountains and walks on the beach: shells, leaves, rocks, and various wildflowers. He made a point to keep the altar very clean, throwing away plants and flowers that became dry and replacing them with fresh ones. His illness made him sensitive to burning incense, so he decided to forgo any aromatic energy enhancements.

Robin is a Christian and has always drawn strength from his faith. Therefore, on his altar he included pictures and figurines of Jesus, Mary, and many of the saints that he had learned about as a child. Each morning and evening, as a part of his ritual of tending to his altar, he recited a specific healing affirmation or prayer, such as,

"My body feels healthy, whole, and energetic. I am radiant with joy and harmony," or *"Give me your blessings Holy Son of God, so that I may behold myself with the eyes of Christ within me and see my perfect health."* He would light a candle, read his daily affirmation a number of times, and write in his journal how he felt about it. Today, he is doing well. He is not completely "out of the woods" yet, but has an amazingly serene and grounded demeanor. He is handling his challenge with tremendous grace and inspiration.

Robin's healing altar

Bathrooms: Worshipping the Holy Body

Bathrooms are associated with water and everything it represents. Washing is a ritual performed by many religions to signify purification, cleansing, and renewal. In Buddhist philosophy, traveling over or through a body of water represents the psyche's transition from illusion to enlightenment. Christians use the ritual of baptism as an initiation into faithfulness, because it is believed that the soul is purified through bathing. Among the Hindus all water is considered sacred, but especially the Ganges River, where people cleanse themselves daily both physically and metaphorically. People also pilgrimage to the shrines in Lourdes, France and Fatima, Portugal to be healed by their holy waters.

It is important to mention here that the energy governing bathrooms is not merely about cleansing. It is about the self-care of your soul, which, for your psychological well-being, requires occasional privacy to one degree or another. Sometimes we need to drop the smile, scratch an itch, cry, and fall apart. Or we need privacy for daydreaming, cogitating, looking at our lives, and simply being at ease. That's when the bathroom is an escape from the pressures of the world. When you are inside and the door is closed, you are usually left alone. No one considers it "open" space to invade.

So allow your bathroom to become a sacred area of healing and renewal. Include the five elements in its décor. Use green plants for Wood, candles and good lighting for Fire (install dimmers), fixtures and towel bars for Metal, ceramic tiles for Earth, and hang pictures of bodies of water, such as seas, oceans, or lakes, for Water. The bathroom has many hard surfaces, such as tiled floors and walls and porcelain countertops, sinks, and toilets. Balance the hardness with softness—soft bath rugs, soft towels, and round soaps and fixtures. To self-nurture, purchase beautifully scented soaps, oils, and lotions made of natural ingredients that resonate comfort and healthy well-being to you.

Feng Shui Bathroom Tips

- Keep your bathrooms simple, clean, and balanced.

- Bathroom doors and toilet lids should always be kept closed in order to prevent positive chi from going down a drain or being flushed away.

- Whenever you can avoid it, don't locate a bathroom in either the Prosperity and Abundance or the Marriage and Relationships zones of your house.

- Similarly, try not to place a bathroom across from the kitchen or the front door. Otherwise you may lose beneficial energy.

Be creative when you are choosing power tools and ingredients for your bathroom. Since this is such an intimate and healing space, think in terms of how your bathroom can renew and nurture you. A sacred ritual can be as simple as having a regular soak in a tub of warm water. For this experience, pour a few drops of your favorite essential oil in the water. Or use something more organic, such as a few buds of fresh lavender. Or keep some fresh rose petals in a glass jar and sprinkle a few in the tub. They will create a special ambiance of soulful nurturing when floating on the top of the water.

The bathroom is a room in which you should indulge your sense of touch. So buy the best quality towels you can afford. Purchase good natural brushes and sea sponges for bathing and cleansing. And, most importantly, keep your bathroom clean!

Tanya's Romantic Spa

Tanya and her family were living in a new home in a new town from which her husband had to commute a long way to work. Because he would often be gone, she was worried that their physical distance might translate into a relationship distance. She planned to use the master bath's intimate environment to enhance the bonds within their marriage, but currently it simply didn't reflect the feeling she wanted to evoke.

The bathroom was configured next to another room that was being used as TV room. Tanya wanted to combine the two rooms into a unified spa zone where she and her husband could explore their romantic impulses and stimulate their senses. Tanya conferred with me in order to identify the ideal feng shui enhancements for creating the sacred sensual sanctuary of her dreams.

Before making any energy enhancements, I worked with Tanya and her husband to determine the smells, mood, colors, and fabrics that resonated with each of them individually. One of the exercises they did was a creative visualization of their fantasy bathing area. They both took a ton of notes. When Tanya and I reviewed these, we came up with a specific list of items for turning the room into an indulgent pleasure zone.

First, Tanya installed a large spa tub in the bagua zone of Marriage and Relationship underneath a big picture window that looked out on a lovely view of the mountains. She surrounded it with lots of pink, white, and red candles. Then, along the wall in the zone of Helpful Friends and Travel, she brought in a low table to make an altar base. On top of it, she placed a large statue of Vajrasattva in union with the Supreme Wisdom Visvatara, a copy of an 18th-century Tibetan bronze statue depicting a lovers' embrace between the deities of Vajrasattva and Visvatara. In Tantric Yoga, couples use the visualization of these two deities to practice merging with the energy of the Divine. Around the room, Tanya also set out a few small candles in holders made of purple glass shaped like lotus flowers, a few pictures of herself and her husband together, and two large crystals. She put two meditation mats and pillows on the floor in front of the altar.

*Vajrasattva in Union with
the Supreme Wisdom Visvatara*

Other furnishings in the spa included a large, comfy chaise longue with pillows for napping, resting, or reading and a massage table. Next to the massage table was a cabinet with open shelves filled with beautiful towels, scented oils and lotions, and two beautiful Japanese robes. Now once or twice a month, Tanya arranges for her husband to receive a massage on Sunday afternoon to invigorate him before his coming workweek. The bath has truly become a sacred sanctuary and she has kept love and joy alive in her marriage.

Home Gyms: Exercising Body and Soul

It is said that the body is a temple for the soul. If so, when we take care of our bodies through exercise, we are also taking care of our mental and spiritual well-being. Pursuing a regular exercise program requires both discipline and mindfulness. Therefore, this kind of activity can be a core element of a strong spiritual practice. Not only is it an opportunity to get in touch with the physical self, but exercise can also be incredibly emotionally de-stressing. If you are one of the few people fortunate enough to have the space for a gym in your home, this, like other rooms, can become a sanctified area. Remember: Where attention goes, energy flows!

Take the case of Kimberly and her musician husband, Josh, who have a large home gym in their basement. It is spacious enough that they can have a small group of close friends over to share a meditation and yoga class, but most of the time, the couple simply uses it alone. The gym is located in the Children and Creativity zone of the bagua in their home, and although they do not have children, this is a sacred space where they devote themselves to nurturing their inner children, or the aspects of their personalities that are innocent, open, and playful. Due to this auspicious placement, they purposefully decided to accent the space with feng shui energy enhancements that would amplify these qualities, thereby fulfilling some of their most basic psychological and emotional needs.

A mirror covers one entire wall, with a ballet barre mounted across it. They wired the light switches with dimmers to brighten or soften the intensity of the lighting depending on whether they were working out or practicing a yoga meditation. On another wall they installed wooden shelving that holds books about exercise and different movement practices, such as tai chi, yoga, and Five Rhythms dancing, yoga mats and straps, small items of exercise equipment, such as hand weights, and a small digital sound system and TV set up for listening to music, following exercise videos, or watching the morning news. This is also the area where they decided to create an altar to celebrate and honor creativity and the inner child spirit.

For the flooring, they laid down commercial carpeting in a muted pale gray tone. They painted the walls a soft white—the color associated with the zone of Children and Creativity. Their various pieces of exercise equipment include a treadmill, stationary bike, stair machine, an upper body nautilus-type machine, and assorted free-weights. They maintained a color tone of whites and grays in the assorted equipment and furnishings, except for occasional highlights of bright purple. The equipment is placed around the room against the walls, leaving the center open as an area for yoga and stretching.

To build their altar, Kimberly and Josh picked out a shelf that could easily be seen from most of the workout equipment. One of their main ingredients is a set of children's bells, one of which Josh has had since he was a baby. It was a christening gift! Whenever they come to the room to work out, they ring these bells to call in their spiritual guidance. They also selected a few of their childhood toys. Kimberly included a doll and a couple of storybooks that she had saved. Josh included some old toy cars and trucks that his mom dug out of the garage for him. One wooden truck was handmade by his cousin and given to Josh for Christmas when he was a little boy. They've opted for no candles, incense, or smudging because they don't want any smoke in this basement area, although they do use an aromatherapy diffuser to subtly scent the room.

Some people also build studios where they can practice what I like to call "spiritual exercise," movement disciplines such as chi gong, yoga, and t'ai chi. These are crosses between home gyms and contemplative environments. If this is your aim, combine the tips below with those in Chapter 8 (see page 155).

Feng Shui Tips for Home Gyms

- Never place exercise equipment in your bedroom. Instead, set aside a special niche in your home exclusively for your workouts.
- Exercise equipment is yang in nature. So balance the room with yin qualities, such as objects or furnishings that are soft and round.
- Weights and machines in a home gym may create an overabundance of "metal" energy. Balance the room with "wood" elements and highlights of "water" and "earth."
- Mirrors should be kept clean. Do not use mirrors that are tiled, faded, or have veins.

A Garden Retreat

The longing to have a garden retreat is a metaphor for life within the Garden of Eden, a setting that calls to each and every person. There are many possibilities for such an imagined outdoor sanctuary. If an area in your garden were meant to be an intimate space, what would be your fantasy or dream about it? What is sacred about your garden? What is your intention for intimacy? In their book *The Sanctuary Garden*, Christopher and Tricia McDowell suggest:

> *"Beyond its practical aspects, gardening—be it of the soil or soul—can lead us on a philosophical and spiritual exploration that is nothing less than a journey into the depths of our own sacredness and the sacredness of all beings."*

Sebastian and Terry's Garden Retreat

Sebastian and Terry have a home in the desert that demonstrates the potential of an intimate garden. It has a small terrace off the master bedroom where they decided to design an intimate outdoor space centering on a spa and swimming pool. In keeping with the local landscape, they created a small oasis of flagstone and boulders. In the evening, they light dozens of candles around the spa, producing an enchanting vision of romance and soothing tranquility, which was their mutual intention.

Sebastian and Terry's intimate spa oasis

The couple adores icons and objects symbolic of the Southwest and the Native American traditions. One of their special feng shui enhancements is a beautiful medicine wheel, about the size of a large pizza pan, made of out of colored pebbles. These are imbedded in the stone paving around the pool, at its exact entrance. They have also placed metal sculptures of the sun and moon near the pool and keep a Native American blanket draped over a wooden bench. Because the couple thought it would be healthful, the plantings in the garden include those considered, by Shamans, to be healing totems. To further emphasize the primal wisdom of their little garden sanctuary, the couple decided to accent the ambient energy by including images and figurines in different media depicting their favorite totem animal guardians: Terry's is the wolf and Sebastian's is the horse.

The hot, dry, sunny desert is most suggestive of yang energy. However, because intimate spaces call for a bit more yin energy than yang, Terry and Sebastian needed to be creative in order to ensure that their sacred sanctuary felt intimate. To this end, they placed big, round boulders around an alcove that was then filled with soft cushions and pillows in dark blue and green colors. They also painted the bottom of the pool black. In addition, they used earthenware pots holding an abundance of flowering plants. As you can imagine, Sebastian and Terry feel their lives are greatly enhanced by their intimacy.

Sacred Burial Sites for Beloved Pets

How many gardens and backyards are out there that have the family's animal companion laid to rest underneath a pretty tree? Our treasured cat, Taj Mahal, had to go to kitty heaven. She was 15 and my sons had grown up with her. Like all pets, she was deeply loved and a true member of our family. So when it came time, we designed a special ritual to guide her departure to the next world. The previous day, my younger son dug a hole in the yard in a place we both liked next to a pond and near a small grove of banana trees.

The vet was kind enough to come to our home and allow us to grieve and say goodbye before he put her down. Afterwards, we held a wake outside in the garden, lit candles and incense, and talked about her little idiosyncrasies. Then we put her in a box, decorated it with colored flowers, and wrote notes expressing her attributes and the things she did which we loved about her. Finally, we put our notes on top of the box and buried her. In the future, we plan to put a pedestal and a gazing ball on this spot as a little shrine to her.

A pet's passing is often one of the more profound and poignant lessons for our children. It's well worth taking the time to weep, talk, and process an animal's death. Having a sacred burial site to visit makes the loss easier to bear and is a beautiful reminder of these special souls. So parents, I encourage you to create your own family rituals when your pets die and to create shrines for them that your kids can participate in building. Consider adding a plaque, memorial marker, or planting a lovely shrub on the spot.

Note: Local zoning regulations vary, so it's best to check the policies in your area. Even if you are not permitted to bury your pet, you can still create a shrine in its memory.

Feng Shui Garden Tips

- Your garden area should be in good repair and free of clutter and debris. Remove dead or dying plants, fix leaking hoses and sprinklers, and mend broken fences and gates.
- Balance the elements of yin and yang. Light and bright areas possess yang energy, shady and cool spaces possess yin energy. An intimate garden calls for an emphasis on yin qualities suggesting quiet, sanctuary, and solitude.
- When you plan to use a garden area as an intimate space, it is a good idea to plant shrubbery or build fencing around this nook to foster the illusion of it being a private sanctuary.
- Harmoniously mix the five elements by combining metal sculptures or furniture with water features like ponds and fountains, ceramic pottery and stones for Earth, red flowers or landscape lighting for Fire, and, of course, plants and flowers for the Wood element!

A Final Thought

Designing an intimate sacred space is a creative process, whether it is an entire room or a small alcove for a shrine. *Webster's Dictionary* defines the word "create" as "to cause to come into existence; to make; to originate." So you start with an intention that answers the question: What do I want to bring into existence? Perhaps it is a practical solution for a physical need, such as a shrine for a deceased pet, a private exercise room, or a nurturing space to tend your body. Or maybe it's a concept from the emotional realm, such as a bedroom that inspires romance and intimacy, or an altar to process an illness and promote healing. An intimate sacred space can also fulfill a spiritual desire, such as getting in touch with your inner child or your divinity. In that case, your intention would be the creation of an area where you could feel safe and secure while going deeply within.

Are you sensing the nearly endless possibilities for bringing your heart's desires into existence in every area of your home? By now, you have surely picked up at least a handful of hints and practical suggestions that you could implement right away. As you begin to create your sacred sanctuary, I hope you'll remember to have a good time and let your imagination freely flow.

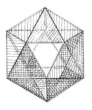

Chapter 7

Zones of Creativity

"What you think, you create. What you create, you become. What you become, you express. What you express, you experience. What you experience, you are. What you are, you think. The circle is complete."

—Neale Donald Walsh, author of *Conversations with God*

Not long ago, I did a consultation for a married couple who are both well-known and talented writers in the entertainment industry. They had already experienced extraordinary success with several films and, after taking some time off and relocating to a quieter town to raise their young children, were now ready to write again. For some reason, however, their creative juices weren't flowing. Could feng shui help?

Their home office was a large and spacious studio off the main house. On one wall was a big fireplace; another featured huge panes of glass looking over a garden and pond. The two remaining walls held floor-to-ceiling built-in bookcases, the shelves of which were so tightly packed with reference materials, files, papers, toys, books, magazines, and games that it looked as though there wasn't a single spare inch to add another piece of paper! Teetering piles of paperwork and books were also stacked up on tables and desks. Clearly, plenty of ideas and words were being generated, but nothing substantial or fruitful. They couldn't seem to put anything together that felt right. Even though they hung out and collaborated in this room, it was stagnant. Nothing was happening.

As they showed me around, I learned that the couple's earlier successes had actually been accomplished outside the home environment. Each day they had gone to a set of offices at a film studio. It seemed fairly obvious to me that their uneasy flow of work could be attributed to the fact that they were now working at home. I asked them to describe their offices from their studio days and compare them to their home office. What felt the same? What felt different? What looked the same? What looked different? It wasn't difficult for them to realize that they needed to declutter in a major way. Most of the "stuff" they had accumulated wasn't necessary, especially since they could use the Internet for research.

When I suggested that they build an altar to reinforce the intention of creating and selling a new film script, they were hooked! They carved out space on some of the bookshelves and built an altar to the "gods of storytelling." For ingredients, they choose awards depicting success. They added a couple of script ideas handwritten on beautiful paper. They painted a colorful mandala depicting their vision of what they wanted from the venture, which they draped above the shelves, and they made a point of keeping several healthy plants and a small vase of fresh cut flowers on the altar.

A mere few weeks after my clients had cleaned out their office and created the writing altar, their creative juices flooded in. The last time we spoke, they informed me that their latest proposal had tweaked the serious interest of several studios.

Zones of creativity are spaces where people work and purposefully create, such as home offices, dens, hobby rooms, artist studios, and children's bedrooms or playrooms. Children are especially good models for creativity because they are constantly learning new skills, expanding their self-knowledge, growing as people, and exploring the world with their imaginations.

Before you read on, take a moment to decide what about creativity is sacred to you. Then, consider the significance of the areas in and around your home that foster self-expression, artwork, and innovation, or any of the other qualities you put on your list.

The Soul at Work

"Work is love made visible," Kahlil Gibran writes in *The Prophet*. Under ideal circumstances, I agree. Work is one of the ways we can express our spirits and make loving contributions to the world. So, if a sense of spiritual service is absent from your work, you may feel a powerful desire to sanctify a workspace in your home. Through work, we exchange gifts of soul and individuality for monetary compensation, but the rewards of working are also intangible. When we give love, we feel loved.

In the last few years, the number of home offices has increased exponentially due to the advances in communications technology. These rooms govern the expression of our divine purposes in the physical world. They also influence the finances of our households because they are where money is generated, managed, counted, worried about, and spent. Considering how important the soul of work can be, it is imperative that your working environment at home adheres to the fundamentals of feng shui.

Once you have chosen a location for your sacred zone of professional creativity—whether that is an entire room or merely an area within a room—the basics of designing it will be largely the same as they are for other kinds of spaces. Specifically, set an intention, do a thorough cleaning, and perform a space clearing ritual. Then, evaluate the balance of energy in your zone and select energy enhancements. Remember, the Wood element rules creative ideas, which are the seeds of new growth. The Fire element embodies careers that require high energy and being in the limelight. The Earth element influences professions dealing with the resources of the earth, such as the building industry. The Metal element fosters careers that pertain to details such as in the sciences and business management. The Water element is characteristic of artists, healers, teachers, and futurists.

Feng Shui Do's and Don'ts for Your Home Office or Den

- If possible, use bookcases with cabinet doors that close in order to keep any negative "cutting chi," caused by the edges of the shelving from pointing toward you.
- **Do** place a fish tank or aquarium in this room to foster prosperity.
- **Don't** position your desk in a direct line with the door, but where you are able to see anyone who approaches the entrance.
- **Don't** buy or use furniture in your office or den from anyone who has gone bankrupt, had severe bad luck, or been through a difficult divorce.

Office Shrines

When creating a shrine in your home office or den, as my clients did to support their scriptwriting process, keep in mind the varieties of potential ingredients that are appropriate for a sacred workspace. Make a point to display your awards, plaques, trophies, and honors. This is also a fun area to include images of a personal totem. So place replicas of your guardian in your office.

In a sense, your desk will always be a shrine because it is dedicated to your success. Arrange items on your desk according to the bagua template. For instance, place your telephone in the zone of Helpful Friends and Travel, which is to your far right as you are seated at your desk. Place symbols of wealth in the zone of Prosperity and Abundance, which is in the top far left corner from where you are sitting. Try a bowl of goldfish, as this is known to foster financial prosperity. Note that the "mouth of chi" will always be positioned at your chair, since this is where chi initially flows into the desktop. Set files concerning your partnerships in the zone of Marriage and Relationship.

Let's take a look at how one person created a sacred home business.

Gabrielle's Healing Center

I consulted with massage therapist and Reiki practitioner, Gabrielle, who lived in upstate New York. She was preparing to transform a spare room on the ground floor of her house into a healing space, where she could develop a private practice and occasionally teach small meditation and Reiki group classes. It was located in her home's bagua zone of Prosperity and Abundance, an auspicious placement, and had wooden floors, a fireplace, and windows on two sides. The door leading inwards opened from a modest entryway located on the side of her house within a small garden. This "mouth of chi" was set in the room's zone of Self-Wisdom and Knowledge, an ideal placement for her clients to initiate their periods of contemplation and inner journeying.

Gabrielle decided to place a large soft area rug on the floor in a pale flowering motif and match it with soft, flowing curtains. She knew she didn't want much furniture to clutter the space. Besides her massage table, she only needed a small desk where she could handle her administrative tasks, shelves to hold her sound system, CDs, and books about healing and spirituality, and three small, round tables to hold altars—one for healing, one for spiritual guidance, and one for abundance. For seating during meditation, she created a cushioned area on the floor in the zone of Marriage and Relationships.

The room had two main feng shui "problems": three long beams extended across the ceiling—a source of negative "cutting chi"—and the fireplace was located in the zone of Children and Creativity—a route for beneficial chi to escape, but the solutions were relatively simple. She added a decorative screen to block the mouth of the fireplace in summer weather, and in the cold of winter she would keep a fire burning there to warm her clients. I informed her that she could hang small crystals or bamboo flutes from the beams to remedy their sharp edges. Instead she draped a flowing lavender fabric along the ceiling. The color was selected to match the pale lavender that she painted her walls. She then hung watercolor artwork featuring angels and scenes from nature.

Finally, because the element of Water governs the healing professions, I suggested that Gabrielle also purchase and maintain an indoor tabletop fountain and a fish tank. It would be important for her to take responsibility for the health and well-being of the fish, just as she would care for her clients and her business. She placed the fish *tank in the area where she collected money and placed the fountain near the entrance to the room. I am glad to say that the last time I heard from Gabrielle she was happy, prosperous, and thinking about expanding her workshop schedule.*

Hobby Rooms and Artist Studios

In her book, *The Artist's Way,* Julia Cameron says that our creative source is in touch with our inner divinity. That's pretty important, isn't it? Yet rooms devoted to artistic endeavors, craft making, and the pursuit of hobbies are often sequestered outside the main areas of the home. If your hobby is gardening, maybe your zone of creativity is in the garden shed. Or maybe it's in the garage, if you're woodworking or building. Perhaps it's the basement or the attic, if you're pursuing arts and crafts. No matter where your zone may be located, making space for creative expression is a sacred opportunity.

It is very sad, but very true, that many of us don't give ourselves permission to create. Or we fail to acknowledge our creativity where it does exist. What have you always wanted to express, but haven't? Are you yearning to have some kind of hobby, or artistic creative outlet? I am. When I began my university degree, I started out as an art major. I loved to draw and paint! Later my path led me away from both activities, but art is an endeavor that I plan to resurrect in the years to come. In the future, I may build an altar dedicated to developing my painting skills. At the moment, I collect pictures of the kinds of paintings that I would like to emulate. They go on my bulletin board.

A Garden Greenhouse

Gardening can be a huge creative outlet. If you have a greenhouse or garden shed, you have a great place to go where you may lose track of time and commune with the Earth's divine elements. In fact, this zone of creativity is a perfect location for a shrine to nature. So, treat your greenhouse like a temple. Hang crystals in the windows to refract light and splash prisms of color everywhere. Place small wind chimes at the door or by a window that can be opened, so they may gently speak to you. Consider installing a small indoor water feature such as a fountain. Fill your shed or greenhouse with found objects that you collect on hikes through the hills or along a beach, such as pebbles, birds' nests, feathers, seashells, and pinecones. And remember that whirligigs, brightly colored flowers, splashing water, and banners are said to attract elemental spirits such as fairies and elves!

A Garage or Toolshed

The garage and toolshed are usually considered the domain of men. These are sacred places for escape from household hustle and bustle, and often become non-spiritual shrines. It is quite possible, that the ability for married men to escape to the garage or tool shed is the saving grace for many relationships. Do you recall the television show *Home Improvement* starring Tim Allen as Tim "the tool man" Taylor? His garage was sacred ground. I imagine one of the reasons for the show's popularity was that many viewers related to his antics involving his garage and tool shop. Men, women, and children all need a place where they can be alone and shut the door.

What might your intention be in the garage? Perhaps it's just to be away from the household for a bit of peace and quiet. Perhaps tinkering with the car or building something is only a pastime. If your interest in cars and building projects is a bit more serious, you may have a more intentional shrine. Remember that a shrine can create itself, evolving over time. It might begin with a toy model car on a windowsill or a shelf. Little by little, other automobile collectibles or car "stuff" can be placed alongside.

My oldest brother Richard liked to tinker with cars as a young man, which led to an interest in car memorabilia over the years. Now he is a well-known collector of unusual and antique "automobilia." When his garage became too small to hold all his "toys" he took over the basement and this space is now his non-spiritual shrine! It is a private sanctuary, where he can take refuge and spend time dwelling within.

Sacred space is for *you*. It is okay to close the door and hang a "Do Not Disturb" sign. Psychologists would agree: However much we love our family, there are times when we need to shut out the world and be alone with our thoughts and creative endeavors.

Feng Shui Tips for Your Hobby Room or Artist Studio

- Display your artwork, crafts, or other creative work.
- Keep art or hobby materials organized and the room clutter free to enhance the free flow of creativity.
- Hang inspirational pieces around your space to influence and motivate you.
- Have a door to your space that you can close for privacy, for when you are "in the zone."

An Artist Crafts an Altar

Greta had an amazing creative sanctuary where she could paint and make pottery. She had built a large room onto the back of her house beneath a huge oak tree. High, vaulted ceilings and lots of big windows made the room appear spacious and full of light. There was adequate room to accommodate all her materials, and plenty of privacy when necessary. When she felt like having company, double French doors led out onto a shady deck where she could receive visitors. The studio also contained a river-rock fireplace that added warmth and gave it an earthy appeal. Overall, it was a magical setting.

Before I met her, Greta had set the intention of taking her painting to the next level. She was in the process of creating a group of related pieces for display in a show. Although she had gotten off to a good start, she was soon feeling drained and oddly uninspired. That's when a good friend suggested that she might be having a feng shui problem and recommended that she contact me.

I must admit that I was very impressed with Greta's studio as I walked in. It was obviously the kind of space and environment any artist would dream of, but I could tell right away what primary feng shui issues were causing her stagnation. To begin with, she had placed her easel right below a ceiling fan. This was causing sharp "cutting chi" to point directly at her while she was working. She was also standing with her back to the fireplace and couldn't see the main entrance without turning around. Furthermore, her fireplace, which was in the zone of Children and Creativity, had nothing in front of it to slow her creative chi from flying right out of the studio.

We got to work. It wasn't too much trouble to move the easel so that she could get out from under the fan and see the door. We placed it catty corner from the door in the zone of Prosperity and Abundance. To solve her other major problem, for the time being we propped one of her paintings in front of the fireplace. But I advised her to get some firewood and to purchase an attractive fireplace screen to place in front of the opening. This would keep her inspiration from floating out through the chimney.

Next, we delved into some deeper significance involved in Greta's creative efforts. The entrance to the studio was located in the area of Helpful Friends and Travel, which was a good placement for having people come to her studio and view her pieces. I suggested she paint the door as if it were one of the pieces in the group. That would attract the type of gallery owners who would be most interested in her work. And I asked her what she wanted to happen in her career as a result of this next show. What was most important to her: selling the bulk of her pieces or becoming better known? That was a tough question for her to answer. She wanted both, of course, but which one did she want most? Greta confessed that she wanted notoriety more than income, so we agreed that this would be her primary intention. We therefore decided to create an altar in the zone of Fame and Reputation. This would be situated next to her work area and across the studio from the doorway, so she would notice it every time she entered her sacred zone of creativity.

After I was gone, Greta first reorganized her studio, cleaning out stale materials and putting old paintings in storage. Then she used bells and singing bowls to cleanse the area energetically and remove old and stagnant chi. She later shared with me that she had found the energy hard to cleanse and move. It had become like old paint adhered to the walls! Eventually, the sound and tone from the bells and bowls rang clear and true and she could feel that the energy had shifted and was flowing. She was ready to select her energy enhancements and gather her ingredients and power tools.

Being an artist, Greta resonated with the finer nuances of color. She was delighted to learn that red was the color associated with the zone of Fame and Reputation. On my next visit, we pulled a long workbench-like table to the wall in that zone and covered it with a pretty, red Indonesian sari that had metallic threads, small beads, and little pieces of mirror sewn throughout it. Propped on the table and against the wall, we placed Greta's most favorite painting to date, figuring that she would put each finished painting there in succession as she completed them. In that way, each painting would be honored and imbued with the energy of creating her Fame and Reputation.

She chose only a few ingredients to place on the table, but surrounded them with an abundance of red candles and incense. These consisted mostly of gemstones, crystals, prisms, and figurines of various goddesses. Greta had a special affinity to the Goddess, who, in many forms, symbolizes the creative force and the act of bringing forth new life.

Now, each day, when Greta comes into her studio to work, she lights candles and incense, and recites a prayer for creativity that she made up:

"Great Mother of Creation, look upon my endeavors today.
Help me trust and surrender to the creative process within my soul.
Bring forth and orchestrate, through me, your love and light,
So that my paintings may be a beacon of beauty
and inspiration to others.
So be it."

An artist's altar bench

Have you ever heard the adage that we are never given a wish or desire without also being given the power to make it come true? That's a hopeful insight, although it does not mean that we can give up working for what we want. In fact, working diligently is part of the "magic" of manifestation. Greta was intuitively aware of this connection.

Through the daily routine and practice of energizing her workspace, Greta's entire art studio lit up with inspiration and creativity. Her enthusiasm and passion returned, and she felt her own goddess energy emerging in her paintings. Now, she is happily looking forward to bringing her inner vision to several more canvases and a local gallery has signed her for a reception and exhibit later in the year.

Children's Bedrooms and Play Areas

Can you recall a time when you were a kid and built a fort in the woods? Or created a tree house in the backyard? Or when your mom and dad helped you build a dollhouse? Or possibly converted an empty toolshed into a playhouse big enough for you and your friends? Wasn't that the coolest thing ever? And while you were envisioning your private sanctuary—during the creation of it—I bet you got lost in thought.

Feng Shui Do's and Don'ts for Children's Bedrooms

- Children should be able to see the entrance to their rooms when they are lying in bed or seated at a desk. **Do** place these major pieces of furniture diagonally from the door, rather than in a direct line with it. Knowing who is coming in helps them to feel secure.

- **Don't** place your child's bed under a ceiling beam ("cutting chi") or beneath a window ("escaping chi").

- **Do** use a combination of stimulating and soothing colors for the walls and decorations in your child's room. For a hyperactive child, limit reds, oranges, and bright yellows and opt for cooling blues and greens or soft pastels. Do the opposite for a lethargic child who needs a boost of energy—emphasize red, orange, and bright yellow.

- **Do** allow children to fix up their rooms in any way they want. Let their imaginations flourish.

- **Do** incorporate plenty of shelving and storage bins in your children's rooms, so they can be organized and easily put things away.

- **Don't** clutter. Like the rest of the rooms in your home, kids' rooms should be clutter-free. Every few years, have them clean out old toys, school work, and other unwanted, unloved, and unneeded items.

Nowadays, when we are timelessly lost in a moment, we often call it a "peak experience." But couldn't it also be called a "peek" experience—a moment when it feels as if we are literally looking into another dimension? That place, where we are suspended in bliss and mindfulness, is the "Now." Children are capable of reaching this state of being all the time, because, in my opinion, they still have a strong connection to the unseen realms.

I believe that it is our responsibility as parents to safeguard our children's precious time to lose themselves in play and imagination. Not only should their bedrooms and play areas be safe places to make believe, explore, and interact with other kids, we also need to foster their abilities here for night dreaming and daydreaming. From the cradle, to the crib, to the twin trundle, to the full-sized bed, as our children grow and get older, we must ensure that the feng shui of these environments supports their individuality and souls.

Shrines for Teenage Souls

With your assistance, allow your teenagers to create their own sacred spaces. They are much closer to the divine realms than we are, thus their imaginations are usually wide open to a vast number of possibilities. In such an adolescent domain, there is often no clear intention of creating a shrine. However, objects may gather spontaneously and a shrine can begin to manifest itself almost magically! If you get the opportunity, reflect on the metaphors and symbols associated with the items that are united in your teens' rooms. This can help you gain insights on the mysteries of their hearts, souls, and psyches.

The teenage daughter of an acquaintance of mine developed the ability to recreate the sacred in a bedroom. Chloe, who was about 13 years old when I saw her bedroom, had created a collage on the wall that her bed was placed against. She had literally covered it from floor to ceiling with pictures and mementos of her life! Three years earlier, she had started pasting pictures on it of camping trips, birthday parties, Girl Scout troop meetings, soccer teams, and classmates, adding to it all the time. By the day of my visit, it included awards, commendations from teachers, ribbons from various sporting activities, poems, pictures from magazines, and an occasional short essay that had received an "A." She was already on her second layer!

I got such a kick out of this incredible shrine to the different aspects of Chloe's life that I giggled when I first saw it. It vibrated with the memories and dreams of girlhood. But because there was so much happening in her collage, I wondered how well Chloe slept at night. When I asked, her mother responded, "Like a baby!"

Another teenager with a noteworthy domain is Lucy and Tyler's son Sean, who is 17 years old. He has taken over the family playroom as a "pad" worthy to accommodate a young man and his pack of pals. Not only is there a bed in it, where he usually sleeps, there is also a "sleeping pit" in the middle of the room for those nights when his friends stay over. Sean manages this bedroom without his parents' interference. Looking around, you can tell that he is a good kid, a good student, and friendly. The room is a shrine to his emerging identity, which is undergoing a rapid transformation.

One whole wall of Sean's bedroom holds stacks of board games, books, and mementos, including a menagerie of every stuffed animal he has ever had since a baby (many of which are beanie babies). Of course, there are also posters of rock bands, cover girls, sports figures, and racecars hung on the walls. He has athletic equipment stashed in the four corners of the room, some musical instruments in one area, a TV with video games on a wall shelf with an old couch in front of it, and a desk space that holds his computer, among other items.

Sometimes children feel a need to hold onto their "things" longer than adults do. Especially as teenagers, their identities can be grounded in their rooms and their "stuff." This is a transformational period when teens are only beginning to find their paths in life. I was excited to hear, from Lucy, that Sean frequently smudges his room. He even collects sage from the local hills to make his own smudge sticks. This is a very good thing—except that one day soon his room will surely be a serious candidate for decluttering!

Creating a Shrine for Your Inner Child

We all have a childhood wound of some kind that we carry with us into adulthood. Although many people are terribly abused as children, I'm not necessarily referring to physical wounds. In fact, the emotional, psychic, and spiritual wounds, such as the fear of abandonment, humiliation, or shame, are often the most pernicious. Until we heal the pain that the child we once were still feels, we lose access to a piece of soul. One of the ways to retrieve the gifts of the "inner child" is through a guided meditation. If you have experienced one, then you probably understand this concept well. I bet it was one of the most moving and poignant experiences of your adult life. It usually is.

No matter what kind of unseen mark was imprinted on you as a child, you can achieve a deep level of healing. Creating an altar or shrine to your inner child may help you reclaim the playful, imaginative aspects of your soul that got lost when you were hurt.

On this altar, place toys, keepsakes, brightly colored objects, and items that are symbolic of your younger years. Spending some time here can help access your imagination.

If you decide to pursue this path of resolution and "soul retrieval," part of your process should be to take an intentional journey to meet your inner child as I described previously. Trust me, your inner child will be delighted that you called upon him or her, and most likely will come running to greet you at the slightest opportunity. Don't be afraid or draw back. Simply close your eyes, relax, and imagine your inner child in your arms or sitting next to you. Stay focused, calm, and attentive. The rest will just flow.

Inner child meditations and soul retrievals are powerful opportunities to reclaim creative aspects of your personality. Because you need all of your ages and stages and joy to be fulfilled through work, play, and self-expression, aren't they worth a try?

A Final Thought

Creative energy is special because it bridges the gap between the conscious and the subconscious minds. Before it can be expressed, or produced materially, every creation must be conceived as a thought, or even a whimsy. Thus creative energy always has an individual stamp on it. It is the force that guides us to dig deep within our psyches, bringing what resides there to the surface, and then manifesting it in the physical world.

If we nurture our children's creativity, they will feel comfortable expressing their individuality later in life. Feng shui offers a framework to explore their likes, dislikes, and soul selves. Remember, creativity can be squashed by adults who have fixed ideas about the way things *should* be. So, let's be flexible in our approach to their personal spaces. If we need to, let's also forgive our own parents and teachers for squashing our creativity.

As I previously suggested, forego any prior thoughts you may have harbored about your own personal creations and what looks "good" or is "appropriate." You are the only one you need to please. As you allow your creativity to flourish, in whatever endeavor you may choose, I believe you'll discover that the energy in other areas of your life that has been blocked or stagnant will be unleashed, too. In essence, your creative floodgates will open.

Chapter 8

Contemplative Environments

"You must have a room or certain hour of the day where you do not know what was in the morning paper ... a place where you can simply experience and bring forth what you are, and what you might be."
—Joseph Campbell

From the moment we get up in the morning to the time we crawl into our beds at night, most of us are bombarded with noise and activity: phones ringing, the television blaring, the clamor of children, or the chatter of co-workers. Sometimes we can "tune out" these distractions; nonetheless they are still affecting us on a subtle level, and often negatively. Thus the opportunity to retreat to a quiet, contemplative sanctuary is a salve that everyone needs upon occasion. Such places are shelters for the spirit. When you are planning one, keep in mind the feng shui principles that produce an ambiance of tranquility and calm, rather than of stimulation and passion. Among other things, contemplative spaces should encourage us to let go of the need for action and accomplishment.

It seems natural that a home would have rooms devoted to sleeping, to eating, to family activities, and to physical well-being. But doesn't there also need to be a room, or an area within a room, that's specifically set aside for the care of the soul? The focal point of this type of sacred space, as in any other, is an altar or shrine. However, in this case it would be used as an anchoring device for meditation, prayer, or contemplation. These spaces offer an antidote to our fast-paced, uncertain, and frequently unsettling world.

As you have already learned, every space has the potential to be sacred space. Most spiritual traditions would acknowledge, however, that to truly engulf yourself in communion with the Divine you must turn your back on your day-to-day world and enter an environment separated from civilization—perhaps a monastery in the mountains or an ashram near the desert. These are quiet, uncomplicated places where meditation, inner reflection, and prayer won't be interrupted, where distractions are minimal, and everything around you supports the spiritual practice of solitude and inner study.

Never fear. Those of us who are unable to completely retreat from our daily lives can still create a sacred room or space for short periods of quiet reflection, stillness, and solitude. Meditation rooms and contemplative gardens are the primary areas in which we can commune with spirit and nature in these manners. Either one may be the most sacred space in, or around, our homes. Such rooms and areas govern the energy of introspection and personal connection to God, Goddess, or All That Is. This includes the place within our selves where the Divine dwells—the heart and the soul.

Meditation Sanctuaries

A Place to Call "Om"

It is not unusual these days for new homes to be built with a sitting room next to the master bedroom. My acquaintance Marta took the sitting room concept to the next level when she created a small meditation room adjoining her bedroom through the bagua zone of Self-Wisdom and Knowledge. How serendipitous! This lovely little sanctuary is painted a warm, golden tone and filled with rose-colored furnishings and accessories. Its central focal point is a tiny fireplace, whose hearth is stocked with a selection of ritual power tools, such as feathers, smudge sticks, and incense.

The room's interior has been decorated both for comfort and beauty. Marta brought in two cushioned chairs, one with a footstool and the other with an ottoman, so that she and a companion can put their feet up when meditating or reading and feel completely relaxed. The fabric covering the chairs is soft, rose-colored chenille. A hand-knitted afghan throw is draped over the back of one of the chairs in case she wants to wrap herself up on a chilly day. Although the room only has one small window, she has positioned a piece of stained glass art in front of it that spreads colored light throughout the room on a sunny day. One wall is covered with shelving on which she has created random altars with pictures and figurines of her favorite spiritual masters, books, candles, and affirmations. Enhancements include crystal balls, a dream catcher hanging by the door, and a chime by the window. On a side table, next to one of the chairs, is another random mixture of books, bells, gemstones, and scented candles.

Because it is so conveniently located, Marta's meditation sanctuary accommodates her contemplative needs in much the same fashion as having an altar in her bedroom would. Morning and evening, she walks by the sacred space as she enters and leaves her bedroom. And since it is so close at hand, it is frequently used. It has gradually become imbued with sacred energy over the years in the same way that sacred energy infuses temples and churches where devotees regularly worship and pray. It is as though an unseen spiritual force has begun to soak, like a liquid, into the walls.

Marta's meditation room

Building Your Meditation Sanctuary

Do all meditation sanctuaries look like Marta's sitting room? No, and it's not required. A kitchen can be a meditation sanctuary, as can a bedroom, or a garden. Our whole lives become a form of meditation and prayer when we practice mindfulness and treat every moment as a spiritual moment. It is worthwhile to prepare your meditation sanctuary to suit your own soul, creating a setting that supports the activities you love and helps you regain your "center" when you wobble.

Once you have found the room or area that "wants" to be your sacred meditative space, cleanse and sanctify the area. During the process of decluttering, keep in mind that it is a good idea to put away objects that may distract you from your soul source. For instance, remove items that have distressing emotional and mental associations, such as paperwork to be filed, and bills, or household projects calling out to you to get done!

Next, evaluate the balance of the five elements: Earth, Fire, Wood, Water, and Metal. Is there just enough of all of them? Do they balance in terms of the yin and yang energy of the space? Contemplative places usually would benefit from an increase in yin energy, so emphasize round, smooth surfaces, soft, relaxing sounds and fabrics, simplicity of furnishings, and subdued lighting. Is there enough natural light, or do you need to add a candle or lamp? Do you have something comfortable to sit on?

As you gather your ingredients, think about creating a focal point—be it an altar or shrine. Remember to choose ingredients that you believe have meaning and connect you to the Divine within and without.

Amanda's Attic Retreat

Recently, I was fortunate to spend a weekend with my dear friend Amanda and her partner, Jack, at their home in the rolling hills outside of the Carmel Valley. They live a quiet and peaceful lifestyle there on a small working farm with a flower garden. A special feature of their home is its attic, in which Amanda has created one of the most magical meditation sanctuaries I have ever been blessed to experience. Amanda is a psychologist by profession and she occasionally allows clients to visit this enchanting mystical abode, but in general it is reserved for her, Jack, and their friends.

To access the attic, you must climb up a pull-down ladder. That places the "mouth of chi" in the floor! Although the room is sort of circular, the entrance definitely opens up in the area of Journey and Career. Therefore Amanda has highlighted this zone with a handmade prayer rug that you kneel upon as you come in. It has a needlepoint design of the "Om" symbol in red on a black background. The color black, as well as the word and symbol, all set the stage for a visitor's "journey" to this upper sanctuary.

Once inside, you can see that Jack and Amanda put sheet rock over the exposed studs in the attic to create walls, and then added lots of shelves. A stained glass window looks out over their pastures and garden. A skylight allows in a good amount of natural light. There is only enough room to sit and crawl, so the floor has soft carpet remnants and lots of blankets and pillows upon which to sit. You would also observe that many different wisdom traditions and beliefs have been honored in this sanctuary.

Amanda feels a special affinity to the Goddess and has numerous figurines and statures depicting her threefold essence, as the Maiden, the Mother, and the Wise-woman, and her many forms in different traditions. These images include several Greek, Egyptian, and Hindu goddesses, the Virgin Mary, and several female bodhisattvas (in essence, someone who has taken the vow to become a Buddha for the sake of all sentient beings). She celebrates the Goddess in the bagua zone of Children and Creativity.

In the zone of Family and Health, she has placed ingredients and power tools from the Native American wisdom tradition and the traditions of other primal cultures. These include drums and rattles, dream catchers, a medicine wheel made out of pebbles from a nearby riverbed, an authentic feathered headdress, handmade rugs and blankets from North, South, and Central

America, and Aztec-like carvings and masks. Since before the Stone Age, indigenous cultures have regarded the Earth as an important figure in the spiritual cosmos. This zone honors Mother Nature through representations of animal totems, feathers, stones, and other treasures from around the farm and garden.

Amanda has placed ingredients in the area of Prosperity and Abundance that reflect the spiritual traditions of the East, such as Tibetan bells, singing bowls, tingshaws, and prayer flags; several depictions of the Buddha and Quan Yin. She has also hung pictures here of honored spiritual masters such as Ramakrishna and Parmahansa Yogananda. In addition, this is the zone in which she has placed several feng shui remedies, such as lucky bamboo flutes with red tassels, a bowl of goldfish, and hanging crystals.

Beneath the stained glass window, in the zone of Fame and Reputation, there is a simple table with an altar cloth that carries a group of red candles in a medley of candleholders of various heights. When Amanda and Jack use the sanctuary at night, they illuminate it solely with these and the scores of white votive candles they've placed around the rest of the space. A ritual practice they often enjoy is to begin a meditation by lighting one or two sage leaves on this altar. A prayer of intention is then read. Soft music is played to complement the meditation. To finish, they ceremoniously ring the tingshaws.

The zone of Self-Wisdom and Knowledge holds a bookcase where the couple keeps their books pertaining to pursuits of body, mind, and spirit. The zone of Helpful Friends and Travel is decorated with Amanda's collection of Christian objects and artifacts—statues and pictures of Jesus, Mary, angels, and several different saints, as well as rosary beads and a collection of antique Catholic prayer books that she has found at flea markets and yard sales. The zone of Marriage and Relationship is dedicated to their relationship. That's where they have chosen to place pictures of themselves as a couple.

Feng Shui Tips for a Meditation Sanctuary

- Do frequent space-clearing rituals and keep the area clutter-free.

- When you sit and meditate, make sure that your back isn't towards the door.

- There are two ideal placements for a contemplative space: the zone of Self-Wisdom and Knowledge and the zone of Helpful Friends and Travel.

- Balance the five elements and incorporate extra attributes of yin qualities to soften the energy of the space, which will make it more conducive to meditation and contemplation.

- Transform a window seat into a quiet alcove for contemplation and reading.

- Decorate a window frame with hanging crystals and prisms that catch sunlight and hang wind chimes nearby to catch the wind.

- Be sure you have a shawl or blanket to keep you warm. Fabrics and textures should be soft and smooth.

- If you regularly sit on the floor, you may want to purchase a traditional Japanese *zafu,* a rather flat pillow that supports the hips and pelvis while allowing the legs to rest comfortably folded.

- Burn incense or a scented candle, or diffuse the air with an essential oil designed for relaxation, such as sandalwood or frankincense.

- Play tranquil music or recordings of soothing sounds. Be sure that extraneous noises are muted and quiet.

- Install a small fountain to provide the relaxing sound of water babbling.

- To imbue the space with gentle energy, opt for pastel colors and subdued shades on the walls and furnishings.

Contemplative Gardens

The ability of nature to enrapture and transform us spans millennia. Spiritual teachers have long taught that there are three main paths of connection with the spiritual realms. The first is through *meditation*. The second is through *service to others*. And the third is through *communing with nature*. The Bible tells the story of Jesus going into the desert for 40 days and 40 nights to commune with nature. When he emerged from his retreat, he began his ministry filled with the power of the Holy Spirit.

Henry David Thoreau, celebrated naturalist and author of the classic *Walden Pond*, made solitude his lifestyle and the wilderness his path. Contemplation enabled him to assimilate nature into his entire being. In his diary, he shared that he could sense water flowing through his veins when looking at a stream, and that "the humming of a gnat is as the music of the spheres, and the music of the spheres is as the humming of a gnat."

Anyone spending quality time in nature can eventually perceive the cosmic order in the pattern of a leaf or the spiraling structure of a seashell. The colors and shapes of flowers, trees and shrubs of the forests, birds and small woodland creatures, the sky, hills, and bodies of water hold countless avenues to access the universal nature of chi. In his book *Inevitable Grace*, Piero Ferrucci writes, "In the contemplation and study of nature, artists of all times—and a number of scientists as well—have extracted from her sounds, shapes, ideas, and inspiration, as though from an immense mine of creative material."

Chi is abundant in nature, so it can be easy to carve out a corner for an inspirational retreat. Although most western architecture and landscape design does not take the natural landscape into account, feng shui's core principles acknowledge the energetic relationship between the landscape, the manmade structures, and mankind's well-being. Gardens, gardening, and gardeners are viewed as a holistic trinity, much like the trinity of heaven, earth, and human beings.

Whether your vision of a garden sanctuary is an ascetic Zen-like environment or a wild, overgrown landscape, your soul knows—and will inform you—if this is where it longs to dwell in the sacred repose of nature and the Divine. You might create numerous kinds of contemplative garden sanctuaries, however there are some universal principles to consider.

- Locate your sanctuary in a spot that ensures solitude. If you're lucky, maybe it's over the knoll beyond the backyard. Or perhaps you have a lovely tree in your yard with a large canopy of branches that can shelter you.

- Ideally, you need to have one wall, fence, hedge, or stand of trees at your back in order to feel supported and protected.

- The outer edges and sides of the space should be lower than the center.

- The pathway to your garden sanctuary should be visible and curved.

- One main feature should be placed at the heart of your contemplative garden sanctuary—something that lures your attention. This focal point—be it an altar, shrine, pond, or view—should stand out from the surrounding landscape.

- A contemplative environment in a feng shui garden should also incorporate the five elements in balance. (This is easier to do outdoors than indoors.)

  - Trees, shrubs, plants, and flowers represent Wood.
  - Boulders, stone carvings, and ceramic pots represent Earth.
  - Fountains, ponds, and pools represent Water.
  - Outdoor fire pits, the sun, and landscape lighting represent Fire.
  - Metal grilles, fences, patio furnishings, wind chimes, and gazing balls represent Metal.

David and Jonathan's Balinese Paradise

Mutual friends referred David and Jonathan to me, as they were in the process of spending a considerable amount of time and money to landscape their garden. Their mutual vision was of a tranquil environment filled with tropical plantings, meandering pathways, and a lovely pond containing large, orange koi fish. They wanted a feng shui consultation to validate the plan, or if necessary modify any aspects of it that weren't auspicious. During our introductory conversation, I asked them, "What specific intention do you have in mind for your garden sanctuary?" For a moment, they had to stop and think about it—they actually had more than one purpose in mind.

We spoke about their lives and careers in order to determine the answer. David runs a large non-profit foundation that provides food, clothing, and medical supplies to people in third world countries who are living under extremely challenging conditions, such as war or famine. Jonathan owns and manages a small software company. He developed and patented a computer program that helps hospitals, doctors, and medical clinics inventory their supplies cost-effectively. Both men are committed to making the planet a better place to live and to personal growth and wisdom. I acknowledged them directly, as they are following a two-fold path to a happy and fulfilling life. One portion of this path is the pursuit of truth; the other is making a contribution to mankind. It was clear to me that the intention for their sacred garden had to include these core values, which they shared. In addition, David and Jonathan occasionally wanted to share their garden with close friends.

Keeping both these factors in mind, and after reviewing their landscape blueprints and walking through the garden with them, I suggested two feng shui areas that could best enhance and support their intentions: the zone of Self-Wisdom and Knowledge and the zone of Helpful Friends and Travel. My suggestion was to create a contemplative shrine in the former and an intimate sacred space with a small table and chairs in the latter.

They started in the zone of Self-Wisdom and Knowledge. Overall their original plans were auspicious. In keeping with the Indonesian ambiance of the garden, they installed a small pond and surrounded it with abundant tropical shrubbery and plants. They filled the pond with lotus blossoms (a symbol of spiritual emergence), water lilies, and goldfish. To one side, they made a little altar with several pieces of flagstone set on top of each other, and built a low, cushioned wooden bench to sit on across from it. Overlooking the pond, were two separate niches. One now holds a stone Buddha in a posture of samadhi

Quan Yin, Goddess of Compassion

"Rocks, willows, lotus pools, or running water are often the indications of Quan Yin's presence. In the chime of bronze or jade, the sound of the wind in the pines, the prattle and tinkle of streams, her voice is heard. The freshness of dew-spangled lotus leaves or the perfume of a single stick of fine incense recalls her fragrance," states John Blofeld in his book *Bodhisattva of Compassion.*

Quan Yin is known throughout Asia as, perhaps, the most beloved of goddesses. Here in the West, she is becoming better known and more popular lately as immigrants continue to bring her image and presence with them. Often referred to as the Buddhist goddess of compassion, it is interesting to note that Quan Yin originally appeared as Avalokiteshvara, a male bodhisattva. His story tells us that he arrived in China from India in the 5th century. For the next 300 years, any depiction of him appeared androgynous. Eventually, early Chinese Buddhists superimposed him and his consort, White Tara, upon each other. They ultimately were melded into one predominantly female entity in the 8th century. Today, Quan Yin can still be found depicted from time to time as a male or an androgynous figure.

Considered one of the few prominent female figures in Buddhism, she is known for her compassionate nature and benevolence. Many women pray to Quan Yin for her intervention in desperate circumstances and as a pathway to mercy, hope, grace, and love.

(Sanskrit for "union"), and the other, a tall ceramic figure of Quan Yin. The results have been magical.

We determined that the zone of Helpful Friends and Travel needed more stone in order to balance the five elements. So Jonathan and

David laid out a flagstone patio, planting tiny white flowers as ground cover between the paving stones. To incorporate the Metal element, they purchased an attractive set of wrought iron patio furniture. To reinforce the Wood element, they also bought a rectangular wooden buffet table to serve as the base of an altar. To balance the Water element, they used blue seat cushions on the furniture. Tall bamboo and banana plants surrounding the seating area provided plenty of sun-dappled shade, generating a soft, yin environment. Terracotta pots filled with flowers represented the element of Earth. In addition, they placed a patio fireplace called a *chiminea*. This introduced the Fire element.

The feng shui enhancements they chose for the entire garden were chimes, colors, and small white lights strung through the trees.

David and Jonathan use their contemplative space in the zone of Self-Wisdom and Knowledge whenever they want to be alone to meditate, read, sit in silence, or relax. They intended this area to be conducive to meditation. But they each have their own rituals before-hand. David likes to begin by lighting a stick of incense and feeding the fish. Jonathan prefers to burn a few sage leaves in an abalone shell that sits on the flagstone altar. They both practice a form of Zen meditation called *zazen*, which is a technique of sitting with the legs fully or partially crossed while breathing silently and rhythmically.

As you can imagine, since both of their careers involve service to mankind, their endeavors often require the assistance of other people. Therefore, other intentions for the zone of Helpful Friends and Travel were to enhance their abilities to contribute and to cultivate friend-ships. Not only did they want to enhance the energy of "heavenly" benefactors, they also wanted to align the help of earthly "angels." In addition, David must sometimes travel to one of the countries his foundation is assisting, and he wanted to ensure safe travel.

Now, David and Jonathan sometimes use the sacred space in the zone of Helpful Friends and Travel to entertain potential benefactors. When they do this, the wooden buffet table doubles as an altar upon which they place bowls of fruit and plates of food amidst many candles and scattered petals from flowers. If it's the evening, they light up the outdoor fire in the chiminea and turn on the little white lights in the trees. Bali high!

Harmony in Nature

In a garden the soul finds harmony with nature—the sun, moon, stars, earth, water, air, minerals, and vegetation. The Garden of Eden is the symbol of what the Bible and some religions call paradise. When mankind "fell" from the garden, symbolically we fell from a state of higher to lower consciousness, from a state of enlightened bliss to the state of unconscious darkness. When we enter a beautiful garden, we are symbolically returned from the darkness into the light. This sensation is inherent whether it is natural and wild, or manicured and orderly. We feel uplifted to our Gaia nature—our cosmic unity with Mother Earth.

Entire books have been written on spiritual gardening (see Bibliography). If you want to dig into creating a sacred space for contemplation in your garden, these can offer you practical information and resources. Here is a suggested process for its creation:

First, always begin by setting an intention. Then take a spiritual journey around your garden and let nature speak to you. Be quiet and listen. It is said that praying is talking to God and meditation is listening to God. This will help you to identify the location in your garden that will enhance your intention. As with David and Jonathan, you may choose a specific zone of the bagua, or you may discover that a certain spot in the garden calls to you. But after you have chosen (or been chosen!), determine the bagua zone it's in. Any zone is acceptable; you simply need to work with them in different ways.

No matter the size of your garden area, I believe there is room to colonize at least a small space for contemplation. Even if you only have a small patio or terrace off an apartment, you can create a nook for communing with your inner spirit.

Next, clear out any dead shrubs and trim overgrown plants. Repair broken faucets and fences, and leaking sprinkler lines and hose bibs. Haul away extraneous debris. You don't want to be distracted thinking about undone garden projects! Then cleanse and sanctify the area by ringing bells or banging on drums.

Note the balance of energy and make a list of anything needed to harmonize the five elements. Is there a shady tree to place a bench underneath? If your space doesn't have any natural shade, can you build or install a small gazebo or create an outdoor tent? Can you install a water feature such as a fountain or pond? Yin energy is shady, cool, and moist. Yang energy is sunny, hot, and dry.

As you begin to gather your ingredients and power tools, remember that a key ingredient is a place to sit. Contemplation takes time, so this is the place to have a "time out." Pick out a chair, bench, or hammock that will be most comfortable. Cushions or a folded up blanket on the seat will help. You don't want to be distracted.

Next, look around and notice if there is a natural way to include a niche, shelf, or platform on which you could build an altar or shrine. David and Jonathan, for instance, created two niches to set statues on. But any kind of table, bench, or shelf would work for an outdoor garden. To form the altar, place your ingredients on your table or shelf. Add pots of flowers and (if there is an electrical outlet) install a small, tabletop water fountain. Add a scented candle and perhaps a talisman or token of your totem animal.

You can make the display as adorned or as simple as the mood suits you. In fact, if you like a simple altar, only add to it when you have a special intention for a meditation. For instance, add a photo of a sick friend for a healing meditation. Or if you are processing an old relationship or mending a broken heart, you may want to add a photo of the person with whom you are completing.

A portable outdoor altar on a tray

Just as David and Jonathan's sacred garden took on a Balinese and Buddhist ambiance, there are a myriad of possibilities to consider if you want to create a space with a certain energetic quality. Here are a few ideas:

- *Fairies and Wildlife:* If you want to attract elemental beings (all fairy-folk creatures) and wildlife, include ingredients such as birdhouses, birdbaths, and splashing water features. In addition, these creatures are said to enjoy gazing balls, whirligigs, banners, and animal totems.

- *Christian:* Incorporate figures of angels, saints, and a statue of Jesus or the Virgin Mary. There are lovely bird feeders made in the likeness of Saint Francis of Assisi, known for his ability to "talk to the birds and beasts." For a monastic effect, hang Celtic wrought iron crosses on a stone wall or fence.

- *Zen:* There is tremendous symbolism in the design of a traditional Zen garden, which is designed to aid in the process of enlightenment. The word Zen means "meditation." The tranquility of these gardens is a result of incorporating the basic principle of feng shui in balancing the energies of yin and yang. If you want to create an authentic one, I would suggest learning more about the subject elsewhere. For the purposes of this book, we can present only basic concepts.

You may want to plant a bodhi tree (*Ficus religiosa*), the tree under which Buddha is said to have attained enlightenment, and, of course, place a statue of Buddha underneath the bodhi. Also consider including a statue of a crane, popular for its totemic powers of grace, longevity, immortality, and serenity. If you like, install a *torii* gate, which, upon passing through, symbolizes leaving the secular and entering into a sacred space. Group rocks in three's, another representation of the Chinese trinity of heaven, earth, and human. Lastly, if you have the space, create a small area of raked gravel that represents both the flow and stillness of water.

Feng Shui Do's and Don'ts for a Contemplative Garden

- **Don't** use pesticides that kill both pests and beneficial insects. You will also be destroying the balance of yin and yang.
- **Do** avoid narrow openings, straight lines, sharp angles, and corners that emit negative "cutting" chi.
- **Don't** let water features become stagnant. Make sure that any water flows towards you rather than away from you.
- **Do** pay prompt attention to any neglected areas of the garden, including seasonal debris, overgrown trees and shrubs, or anything that is broken.

A Final Thought

A contemplative environment may be a spiritual oasis at the end of a busy day or it may be the platform upon which you greet the dawn. Most of all, it will be a setting where you can celebrate the presence of the sacred within yourself on a regular basis. Although any space for meditation, prayer, or spiritual exercise can be seen as a vehicle to access the soul, since the subconscious mind recognizes consistency, it is best to establish a regular time to shut out the rest of the world and turn your consciousness inward.

By now I hope you are well on your way to establishing the sacred home sanctuary of your dreams. Most importantly, it is time to live the life that you have envisioned leading in this space. In the next, and final, chapter of this book, we'll look at rituals and meditations you may enjoy practicing in your sacred spaces to empower your intentions.

Chapter 9

Sacred Rituals

"*We are what we think.*
All that we are arises with our thoughts.
With our thoughts we make the world."
—*The Buddha*

My writing partner, Stephanie, greets every morning by spending 20 minutes seated on a forest green zafu and zabuton meditation cushion set in front of her living room altar. When she first began meditating 12 years ago, she practiced Tibetan Buddhist style, using a mantra. Now her daily ritual is eclectic, although she still finds that she can go deepest into her inner realms when she holds the formal posture that she originally learned. It has become ingrained in her nervous system. Depending on what's going on in her life she may pray, chant, do patterned breathing, meditate, or perform *distance healing*—sending light and love to people in need. When asked to describe her process, she jokes, "You might call it meditation or prayer, but to me it actually resembles a negotiation. I definitely feel the need to offer my spirit guides input and feedback."

Stephanie's altar is a hexagonal wooden table located in the Self-Wisdom and Knowledge zone of the bagua. Its ingredients change frequently, although a peaceful wooden Buddha and a cast metal jaguar from Indonesia are always stationed on the easternmost edge, with a candle, incense, and offering dish in front of them. When her mother recently broke her ankle, Stephanie added her mom's photograph and transformed her altar into a focal point for healing energy. When our earlier book *Exploring Feng Shui* was initially published, she hosted a gathering and invited those who attended to place blessings for the book inside a large glass vase in the center of her altar, thus transforming it into a focal point for abundance. Often she places ingredients on her altar that purely remind her of a free-flowing sense of beauty, joy, and spiritual grace.

The art of feng shui is a metaphor for the dynamic relationship between heaven and earth. Thus when you are using your sacred sanctuary or altar, you are developing a more intimate personal relationship with God, Goddess, the Creator, or whatever name you prefer. Your ritual acts of prayer, contemplation, and ceremony are opportunities to connect with this Source and draw its divine energy into your life. These practices form the framework of a co-creative partnership in which you share your most heartfelt intentions with the understanding that you will be guided and led to manifest them.

In this final chapter of the book, we'll explore some of the ways you can activate the energy of your altars, shrines, and sacred spaces on your own, with a partner, or in groups. You've already seen me refer to different rituals in earlier chapters, although (with a few exceptions) not in as explicit detail as here. Space clearing is a ritual, for instance, as are celebrations of life transitions, such as engagement dinners and bridal showers. So are meditation and prayer, but so, too, can be an ordinary activity such as washing the dishes. Rituals are acts of empowerment that connect us to what is sacred. They can help us to transform, heal, grieve, renew our balance, and offer gratitude.

Meditation and Mindfulness

What is the purpose of meditation? To still the mind and the body, and tune in to the intuitive higher self that resides within, and also, to become mindful of the present moment. Usually the instructions for a meditation are simple and yet many people have trouble putting this concept into practice. Something in them resists it. If you're a person who has trouble sitting still, I recommend learning a moving meditation, such as yoga or tai chi, instead of a seated practice. Either way, the aspiration is to become so focused that tranquility and clarity of thought can be retained even in the midst of chaos. There is a sense of neutrality in this stillness that is extremely potent. But this is something accessed only by training the mind for a while. So, give it a chance before you give up.

Buddhist meditation teacher Jack Cornfield, author of *Buddha's Little Instruction Book,* says: "We may start by practicing meditation much like practicing the piano. Eventually, when we become proficient, we will not need to practice anymore. Just as practice becomes playing, everything we do will become a meditation." Contemplative, emotionally nourishing activities, such as reading, drawing, prayer, writing, or listening to music, can be viewed as meditations, so long as we approach them with mindfulness.

Here are a few different ways to meditate. Perhaps one will resonate with you.

Meditation on the Breath

To breathe is to be alive. Breathing is a primary rhythm of the body, a ceaseless tide of inhalation and exhalation. Since it has two equal parts, one of the simplest ways to meditate is by focusing on your breath. When we feel angry, nervous, or frightened, the breath tends to become faster, shallower, and more erratic. In sleep or relaxation, it is slow, steady, and deep. Putting your attention on the breath can help you become more mindful of your emotional state, physical tension, and mental activity. You can do this form of meditation anywhere, anytime, and for however long you like. Most people who meditate, however, report the greatest benefits from committing to a regular practice schedule, such as 20 minutes before they begin their day or 20 minutes before they go to bed.

Once you begin to meditate, you may find that you have been largely unaware of your extraordinary amount of tension and near ceaseless mental turbulence. For a while, you may even drift off to sleep every time you meditate. That's okay. It only means you are coming into balance. Later it won't happen so frequently. As the process becomes more familiar, you should find that it gets easier to sustain your concentration for the duration of the meditation. Here's how to do it:

Begin by sitting comfortably in a chair with your feet flat on the floor. Your spine should be as erect as possible, so you may want to place a cushion behind your lower back for support. Let your hands rest palms up or palms down on the tops of your thighs. Your head should be very slightly tipped forward and your jaw should hang loose.

An option is to lie on your back in what yoga practitioners call the "corpse position," with your legs spread slightly apart and the palms of your hands facing the ceiling. The one drawback of a reclining position is that it can encourage sleep, which defeats the purpose of the practice. To enhance mindfulness, it is preferable to remain conscious throughout your meditation—unless, of course, you have a strong need for rest.

Close your eyes and breathe naturally through your nose. Place your attention on the air that is entering and leaving your body and the sensations it is causing. Follow the stream of each inhalation from where it first contacts your nostrils, to the back of your throat, to your trachea, and perceive how it expands your chest and belly. Then follow it as it reverses direction, collapsing your belly and chest and leaving your nostrils.

Continue with the next breath, and the next, and so on. See whether you can get as specific as following a single molecule of air. Whenever you find your mind wandering, simply bring your attention back to the breath. That is the extent of this practice.

Concentrating on a Word, Phrase, or Sound

You can also meditate by selecting a word, phrase, or sound upon which to place your focus. In eastern spiritual traditions, going back thousands of years, this is known as a *mantra*. During this type of meditation it can help to use a two-syllable word or phrase to match the rhythm of your breath, although it is not essential. It is most important that the mantra is meaningful to you, perhaps a quality you wish to cultivate or experience.

Many people use the name of a spiritual teacher they admire, such as Buddha, Jesus, Mary, or Gandhi, for their mantras. The Sanskrit language is composed of universal sounds that may also be combined into different mantras that are purported to change your internal vibration through the principles of resonance. A common Sanskrit mantra usable by anyone is "So Ham."

Once you have chosen your mantra, here's how to do a meditation:

As in Meditation on the Breath, begin by sitting comfortably in a chair with your spine erect and supported, or by lying on your back with your legs slightly apart and your palms facing the ceiling.

Close your eyes and breathe naturally. With each inhalation, in your mind silently repeat the word or phrase you have selected, such as: "Love" or "Health." Allow yourself to be filled with the meaning and sound of the mantra. Whenever you find your attention wandering, gently guide your focus back to the mantra.

Mindfulness in the Kitchen

Your kitchen can be an ideal place to explore your spirituality. Mindfulness, the discipline of being fully present in the moment, is a form of meditation easily practiced during the preparation of meals and the cleaning of your kitchen. The instructions are simple: Wherever you are, be there totally. Pay complete attention to every detail, whether you are chopping vegetables or frying an omelet. Just have the experience. In the process, you'll find that you have become more deeply rooted in your sense of aliveness.

In his book *Peace Is Every Step*, renowned Vietnamese Zen master Thich Nhat Hahn shares his viewpoint on washing dishes:

"To my mind, the idea that doing dishes is unpleasant can occur only when you aren't doing them. Once you are standing in front of the sink with your sleeves rolled up and your hands in the warm water, it is really quite pleasant. I enjoy taking my time with each dish, being fully aware of the dish, the water, and each movement of my hands. The dishes themselves and the fact that I am here washing them are miracles! I must confess it takes me a bit longer to do the dishes, but I live fully in every moment and I am happy. Washing the dishes is at the same time a means and an end—that is, not only do we do the dishes in order to have clean dishes, we also do the dishes just to do the dishes, to live fully in each moment while washing them."

Prayer and Contemplation

To imbue your sacred space, altar, or shrine with a powerful boost of energy and life force, include prayer in your daily rituals and usage. God "hears" us through our heartfelt prayers. (There's an old adage that prayer is talking to God and meditation is listening to God.) Fortunately, it doesn't matter exactly how you pray—you can pray in any language or by using words taken from the prayer book of any religion. It also doesn't matter where you pray—you can pray while walking to the store, lying in bed at night, or on your knees in a cathedral. And, as far as I'm concerned, when you pray is up to you. All that matters is that you put both your heart and mind into the words (or thoughts) you do use.

In his book *The Isaiah Effect*, scientist and peace activist Gregg Braden described how there is a knowing or feeling-ness to prayer. He tells a story about a Native American friend, a rainmaker who prays to offer thanks for *what is to be*, as though it already *was*. His prayer was to experience the rain through all his senses: what it looked like, sounded like, felt like, tasted like, and smelt like—and release the image with gratitude.

SUMMONING THE ARCHANGELS

It is said that people can summon, or evoke, the presence of angels through various means in order to request their divine assistance. Try the following prayer and feel free to substitute your own words as you feel so moved. Several participants at the beginning of a group ceremony can also do this. Simply substitute the word "we" for "I."

Begin by taking a moment to breathe deeply in silence. Imagine that you are encased in a bubble of golden light that is safe, warm, loving, and nurturing.

Now, face East and say, "I invite Uriel's presence to join me. Please give me clarity and show me how I can be of service right now." Spend a moment in reflection.

Next, turn to face South and say, "I invite Raphael's presence to join me. Please give me healing and show me what I can let go of in my life right now." Again, reflect.

Then, turn to face West and say, "I invite Gabriel's presence to join me. Please give me strength to overcome my fears right now." Spend a moment in silence.

Finally, turn to face North and say, "I invite Michael's presence to join me. Please grant me wisdom and love and show me what I am ready to learn right now." Again, spend a moment in silent reflection.

Afterwards, sit for a time and contemplate. Remember to offer your thanks.

Saying Grace

Saying grace at mealtimes and special occasions is a time-honored tradition. Prayers, poems, songs, and inspirational messages not only give thanks for the meal and food, but also imbue those gathered with increased love and life force. When you use your altar or shrine, pretend as though you are sitting down to a wonderful meal and gathering of your family and friends and begin by saying grace. This can be a prayer, poem, or affirmation with which to begin any ritual. Say grace again in closing your ritual. What you do, think, and say will infuse and amplify your intention.

There is modern scientific evidence that suggests that thoughts and words have a powerful impact on our bodies at the cellular level. A Japanese researcher named Masaru Emoto photographed frozen crystals of water, formed after being exposed to spoken words and written messages. "Love and appreciation" and "Thank you" produced harmonious patterns. Whereas, "You make me sick" and "I will kill you" produced irregular and disrupted looking crystalline forms. Since the human body is largely composed of water, we can extrapolate that beneficent phrases and concepts are healthy focal points, nutrition for our cells and souls.

Feng Shui and Rituals

There isn't much mention of rituals in the application and principles of traditional feng shui, except for the ritual of space clearing. Feng shui does, however, stress the importance of setting intentions when you are cleansing and applying feng shui cures and remedies. So how do we suffuse and activate an intention? It is my belief that we activate and magnify our intentions when we repeatedly invoke them while in a state of heartfelt awareness—during rituals.

Mind you, a ritual can be a silent prayer or affirmation, or it can be a more elaborate physical "doing" of an action, such as lighting a candle, ringing a bell, chanting, or dancing. Always remember: When using your sacred spaces, altars and shrines, amplify the ambient energy by uniting heart, mind, spirit, and body with rituals.

Rituals for the Changing Seasons

No matter where you travel, the changing of the seasons is celebrated. There is a primal human recognition of our dependence on the natural environment for survival. As we evolved into agriculturally oriented civilizations, although we maintained a sense of awe we began to cultivate an understanding of nature's mysterious forces. In the Introduction, I briefly described the origins of feng shui in China as a discipline to harness the energy of the elements for the benefit and safety of the people. The earliest practitioners knew that, within our lives, there exists patterns of birth, generation, destruction, and rebirth that are reflected in the cycles of the seasons. And so do spiritual leaders in other cultures.

There are definitive times, throughout the year, when performing rituals can truly activate the energy of certain kinds of intentions. This fact is accepted by many traditions. You can empower yourself by setting aside a day or evening to join with family and friends—or to solo—in a ritual orchestrated to coincide with a solstice or equinox.

Spring

Spring represents rebirth, renewal, and the spark of potential. It is the best time to release old, stale patterns and initiate projects and relationships. You may not realize it, but "spring cleaning" is a potent annual ritual. Open up your windows, do a space clearing, and set an intention for the year ahead. Seeds that were lying dormant in the frozen soil are sprouting tender, pale green shoots to climb upwards toward the sun. So are you!

In Christianity, Easter is the spring holiday that commemorates the rising of Jesus from the tomb. It signifies eternal life. Many families attend religious services and host large meals. In homes with small children there are hunts for colorfully painted eggs, hidden indoors and outdoors. Decorative baskets are prepared filled with goodies. In Judaism, the spring holiday is Passover, commemorating the ancient Israelites fleeing from Egypt. A Seder is held where participants recount the story of the Exodus and symbolically recreate elements of the telling, such as by eating bitter herbs and *charoset*, a paste of spices, wine, matzo bread, and fruit. Children hunt for a hidden piece of matzo recalling hunger in the desert and divine manna that fed the people. In Wicca and Celtic Shamanism, the spring equinox represents a day of light and dark in perfect balance. It commemorates the return of the Divine Mother Goddess.

Create a simple spring ritual by having guests bring one flower of any kind to your home. Place these in a beautiful vase on an altar prepared with a green altar cloth, green candles, and living plants. If you wish to include a crystal or gemstone, select one that's green, such as an aventurine. Also set out a bowl of holy water.

During the ritual, have all the participants come forward one at a time and sprinkle themselves with holy water for purification. Then have them light a candle to affirm something new they desire to manifest in their lives—a job, improved health, greater intimacy—stating their intentions out loud. Finally, have them take a flower out of the vase (a different one from the one they each brought), to symbolize their intentions flourishing and beautifully enriching their lives.

Summer

Summer is a time for communal events and celebrations. The early months relate to marriage, fertility, and abundance. It's not hard to recall that life-affirming sense of freedom we had as kids on summer vacation either. This is the season for outdoor activities such as backyard barbecues, picnics by the seashore, water sports, and hiking in the woods. Because the days are longer, by the time the sun drops beneath the horizon, people seem to emanate a dreamy, tired energy of joyful surrender.

Create a summer ritual of joy, freedom, and fellowship by gathering a circle of friends around a bonfire at sunset in the sacred space of your backyard. (Of course, you'll need to be careful and take the necessary safety precautions.) If you're lucky and live on a beach, this is the best site for a flaming event. Ask the participants to bring drums, rattles, and other instruments. As the music begins to flow, those who wish may dance freestyle in the center, following the dictates of their souls. An altar to the "gods of play and laughter" can be built to one side of the fire pit, upon which people can place a token of their favorite activities. Once the musicians are through playing, everyone will settle into a circle and take turns telling stories and jokes. Feasting and merriment should ensue.

Autumn

Autumn is the season of the harvest and the departure of the sun. It is a time of gathering in, contraction, and preparing for a more internal, cocoon-like period. The equinox, again, is a day of perfect balance, but this time the "shadow" is rising. Here, in America, we make a sacred stand against the impending darkness by celebrating Thanksgiving.

Consider making a ritual offering to Gaia, the Earth Goddess, in gratitude for the circuitous exchange of energy from the earth, to your body and soul, and back to the earth. Begin by gathering the following ingredients from your kitchen and arranging them together on a breadboard or an attractive plate or tray, which will become your table altar.

- Fresh produce, such as tomatoes, carrots, and corn.
- Freshly cut herbs from your own herb garden.
- A yellow or orange candle, symbolic of the leaves.
- Freshly peeled lemon rind, to uplift the ambient energy.
- A utensil you often use for cooking.
- A piece of bread, symbolic of nourishment.

As the meal begins, light the candle and have everyone place the palms of their hands above the food. Together, invoke out loud:

Mother Nature (God or Spirit),
May peace enter our hearts as we consume this meal.
We ask you to bless this food.
Give it healing and nurturing powers
Imbued with love and vitality.
We are grateful for your bounty.

Then, have everyone join hands. In turn, people will say one thing they appreciate about themselves, one thing they appreciate about the person to their right and one thing about the person to their left, and then state what makes them feel grateful in their lives. At the end the circle of people will lift clasped hands, stamp one foot, and exclaim: "Ho!"

Winter

Have you ever seen that popular cartoon of the "old year" as an elderly gentleman wearing a tuxedo and top hat hunching over a cane, and the "new year" as a cherubic baby sporting a diaper? That about sizes it up. Winter holidays typically celebrate the passing year and our hopes for a bright future. Because this solstice is the shortest day of the year (the spring solstice possesses the shortest *night*), we generally understand that things can only get better!

In Rome, they used to have Saturnalia at this time of year. The Egyptians held a similar celebration honoring Isis and her son Horus. In 350 A.D., Pope Julius declared that the birth of Christ would be celebrated at the same time as these other solar deities. The concept behind them all is resurrection and the divine illumination of the world.

Have a caroling party as a ritual celebration. Find a good hot drink recipe (preferably one full of rum!), fill a giant punch bowl with it, and invite your neighbors, friends, and family over to join in. Hang strands of tiny lights bulbs everywhere. Let children decorate gingerbread men. Sing your hearts out!

Rituals for Zones of the Bagua

As we learned in Chapter 1, Identifying Your Sacred Space, each zone of the bagua governs an area of life experience. If you have combined your intention with the correlating bagua zone for your sacred space, it would be very beneficial to conduct a specific ritual that will inherently boost the energy of your intention. Using the zone of Journey and Career as our example, let's take a look at how you could do that.

Perhaps you have the intention of seeking a new purpose for your life and you have created a table altar in the zone of Journey and Career to manifest your desire. You have chosen various ingredients and power tools, such as prisms of cut glass, a dark blue candle, a small indoor fountain, and a small picture of the sea. You can design a short ritual like the one below. Add to it as your mood or tastes suit you.

To prepare, create a treasure map that outlines your new life purpose (see p. 98). Make it small enough to fit on your altar, say on an 8" x 11" piece of cardboard. Leaf through magazines and periodicals, cutting out pictures, words, and phrases that inspire you. After you have glued the pieces to the board, place it on your altar. Then, each day, take a few minutes in the morning and at night to activate it with a ritual as follows:

Begin by clapping your hands loudly three times. Light the candle on your altar. Look over your collage, focusing intently on each picture, word, and phrase. Feel the imagery and sensations that your new life purpose brings you. Stay focused. When you are finished, close your eyes and say a prayer or affirmation, such as: "May the will of the universe be done." Open your eyes, blow out the candle, and let go of any attachment.

To determine which zone of the bagua might be ideal for a specific ritual intention, review their meanings in Chapter 2, Identifying Your Sacred Space.

A music altar for the bagua zone of Children and Creativity

Rituals for Life Transitions

Life is a journey filled with exciting, challenging, and rewarding times. Celebrate these life-changing transitions with rituals and celebrations, for they can ease a difficult experience or enhance a happy occasion. As previously mentioned, you can do these with family and friends, or alone, if that suits you and the situation best.

Birthdays

A birthday is a celebration best shared with family and friends, and it's a good time to create an altar on your dining room table. Not only for a party on your special day, but also for the following week. A yellow altar cloth will uplift and boost the energy of joy and happiness. Brightly colored balloons and party favors, such as hats and noisemakers, are fun and upbeat ingredients, too. Cake is a traditional party food, so be sure to have one in the middle of the altar, with a few small candles on it. Invite those people closest to you over and ask them to bring a memento or item to put on the altar that reminds them of shared good times with you. Also, include photos of you from other birthdays and ages.

To begin the ritual, ask participants to form a circle around the table holding hands. One by one, allow people to note their contribution to the altar and the story behind it. Then have them tell you what it is about you that they love and cherish. After everyone has spoken, you can say a few words to the guests as well. Sing the traditional "Happy Birthday" song. Then, light the candles on the cake, make a silent wish, and blow out the candles. Cut the cake, eat, drink, open gifts, and enjoy!

Getting a New Job or Beginning a Project

That first day of work can be both exhilarating and anxiety provoking. I have a friend who always gets a low-grade fever when she starts a new position, which is troublesome since she's a temp! Energetically, the first day on a new job sets a whole pattern into motion. Thus this transitional moment should be handled in a respectful, mindful manner. I recommend establishing a prosperity altar in your home that you can attend for one full lunar cycle. The transiting of the moon in this circumstance represents the whole tenure of your job.

Build the altar with a purple altar cloth; purple candles; amethyst crystals; work-related animal totems, such as the buffalo, elk, or fox; personal symbols; and images of prosperous people in your field. As a ritual, light a stick of frankincense. Dab your temples and wrist pulse points with a hint of vertivert essential oil. Then read an abundance affirmation out loud, such as:

- ◆ "I am abundant, joyful, and productive."
- ◆ "I am willing to thrive and be prosperous."
- ◆ "I am talented and intelligent, and people recognize it."

You might also consider building an inspiration altar. Use a blue altar cloth; blue candles; and blue gemstones, such as lapis lazuli or sapphire; winged totem creatures, such as the butterfly; personal symbols; instruments of your field of endeavor; and images of wisdom figures. As a ritual, light a stick of sandalwood incense. Dab your temples and the wrist pulse points with orange essential oil. Read inspiring affirmations. Later, make a point to honor the energy you have activated by setting a vase of fresh flowers or a living plant upon the altar.

Graduation

Graduating from school, no matter what the age or grade, is both an occasion to celebrate and honor an accomplishment and a rite of passage. Celebrating the completion of college or vocational studies is not just a completion, for instance, but also the start of a new part of life. Young and old alike gain self-esteem from knowing that they have completed a long, and sometimes arduous task.

A good placement in the bagua for your graduation altar would be the zone of Self-Wisdom and Knowledge. This area governs personal development and scholarly academics. Presuming that you desire to honor your accomplishment with family and friends to support you, design a ritual like the following:

Arrange a table in the area of Self-Wisdom and Knowledge in the room. As a gift, ask each guest to bring a book or item that pertains to the subject of your studies. Cover the table with a blue cloth. Place a blue candle, the gifts, symbols of the area of study, and a bowl of fruit to symbolize bounty on the table.

To begin, ring some bells or tingshaws and light the candle. Have the guests tell the graduate how happy and impressed they are on this occasion of graduation, why they think he or she will do well at his or her chosen area of study, and how they will support the graduate in future endeavors. Close the ceremony with the graduate sharing a little about what they learned and thanking each guest for their support. Clapping and toasting are most appropriate at that moment!

Marriage

Many couples make a romantic gesture of marrying each other in a private ritual. This occurs before a religious leader formally, publicly, and legally marries them. If this is your preference, try the following ritual recipe:

To create a *marriage altar*, prepare a foundation with a rose-colored altar cloth or a carpet of red rose petals. Set two red candles on opposite sides of the altar and a bowl of ripe, colorful fruit in the center. You and your beloved should each prepare a small wrapped gift that holds a personal token or precious symbol, such as a lock of hair, a small quartz crystal in the shape of a heart, or a photograph from childhood, which you will give to the other. You will also need patchouli essential oil.

Begin by holding hands and gazing into each other's eyes. Ask your guardian spirits to join you. Each of you should then anoint one of the candles with patchouli oil and light it, placing it back where it was. Hold hands again. One of you will now offer the other a gift, saying:

"I freely give you my love for now and always."

The other, upon receiving the gift, will say:

"I receive your abundant love into my heart for now and always."

Then, simultaneously, move the candles you've lit into the center of the altar so they are touching. In unison, say three times:

"We marry."

Finally, eat from the bowl of succulent fruit. Let the candles burn until they merge.

Divorce

Just as we need to celebrate the joining of souls and destinies, we also need to honor the souls of our partners when our life paths forge in separate directions. In her book *The Joy of Rituals*, Barbara Biziou describes a simple ritual for a couple that is divorcing to resolve the experience emotionally. Both participants prepare by getting clear of what their union has signified to them, and then they meet in a neutral place and exchange this information in a respectful manner. Before beginning they light a candle, which is then symbolically extinguished to conclude the ritual. The final act of dissolution is burying the wedding rings or tossing them into a body of water.

Birth

Many cultures have naming ceremonies for newborn babies. The purpose of these is to welcome the child into the tribe or community, and in some cases to bring the newborn into the fold of a religious faith. In certain Native American nations a baby might be passed around from hand to hand and literally greeted. The parent or grandparent lifts the baby up and states his or her name so that there may be soul recognition. When the child is of age, it is possible for them to select a new name representative of qualities that they emulate or talents they have exhibited for the benefit of the collective.

Consider hosting a naming ceremony for your infant child. It should include generations of family members and friends. Perform activities and incorporate objects that signify the introduction of a whole and unique person to these loving caretakers, who are willing to participate in the child's upbringing.

Death

When my father died, my mother was bereft and asked my brothers and I to host an Irish wake for him at her house. Everyone they knew came over, bringing tons of food to celebrate his passing. We spread old photographs and newspaper clippings of Dad from every circumstance and stage of life—boyhood to adolescence to adulthood, and in local theater productions—around the dining room table and spent hours telling stories and memorializing him. We even sang "Oh Danny Boy" and drank a toast. One of the best things about the occasion was the comfort it brought my mother. Death is a natural passage, but the mourning process is not always easy to go through on your own.

There are many times when we need to grieve. People die, pets die, and friends move away, or a stage of our lives has "died." This is the cycle of life. With ritual we can embrace these moments, draw deeper connections to the meaning of what and whom we hold dear, and find the fortitude to go bravely forward. So, death is a great teacher, and one of its lessons is about what is valuable. It is vitally important to acknowledge someone who has passed away and all that they've contributed to the world in order to accept their transition. Although they are no longer present in the physical realm, their soul energy still resides within our hearts and memories.

Conclusion

In this chapter and in this book, I have only been able to scratch the surface of the magic of feng shui, the sanctity of the home, and living a lifestyle aligned with your soul. You now have a vast array of knowledge and tools at your disposal—enough to get started. Still I encourage you to explore, observe, read, and otherwise research anything in the world and in your home that plucks at your heartstrings.

Approach the process of *Creating Home Sanctuaries* as an innocent child at play. Trust yourself. You know what feels good and appropriate. This is about delighting your senses, comfort, stimulation, attaining balance and health, and celebrating life. Your aim is both to get in touch with your inner spirit and to access the Divine realms. After reading this book, I hope your imagination is on fire with possibilities to enrich your environment, your relationships, find peace, and realize your dreams—whatever they may be. Your home is a sanctuary for your journey today and in the future.

Remember: Always tune in to your heart and listen to your inner wisdom. Set clear intentions and make loving choices to support and honor them. There is a divine spark within you that has the power to illuminate the world.

Go forth and shine!

Bibliography

Alexander, Jane. *Rituals for Sacred Living*. New York: Sterling Publishing, 1999.

——. *Spirit of the Home*. New York: Watson-Guptill, 2000.

Andrews, Ted. *Animal-Speak*. St. Paul, MN: Llewellyn Publications, 1993.

Arcati, Kristyna. *Gems and Crystals*. London, England: Hodder & Stoughton, 1994.

Bizou, Barbara. *The Joy of Ritual*. New York: Golden Books, 1999.

Blofeld, John. *Bodhisattva of Compassion*. Boston, MA: Shambhala Publications, 1988.

Bowker, John W. (editor). *The Oxford Dictionary of World Religions*. New York: Oxford University Press, 1997.

Budilovsky, Joan and Adamson, Eve. *The Complete Idiot's Guide to Meditation*. New York: MacMillan, 1998.

Chiazzari, Suzy. *The Complete Book of Color*. Dorset, UK: Element Books, 1998.

Cruden, Loren. *The Spirit of Place*. Rochester, VT: Destiny Books, 1995.

Curott, Phyllis. *Book of Shadows*. New York: Broadway Books, 1998.

Ferrucio, Piero. *Inevitable Grace*. New York: J. P. Tarcher, 1990.

Hahn, Thich Nhat. *Peace Is Every Step*. New York: Bantam Books, 1991.

Jordan, Michael. *Encyclopedia of Gods*. New York: Facts on File, 1993. Out of Print.

Lawlor, Anthony. *A Home for the Soul*. New York: Clarkson Potter, 1997.

——. *The Temple in the House*. New York: J.P. Tarcher, 1994.

Lawson, David. *The Eye of Horus*. New York: St. Martin's Press, 1996.

Leidy, Denise Patry and Thurman, Robert A.F. *Mandala*. Boston: Shambhala Publications, 1997.

Linn, Denise. *Bringing Sacred Shrines into Your Everyday Life*. New York: Ballantine, 1999.

——. *Feng Shui for the Soul*. Carlsbad, CA: Hay House, 1999.

——. *Sacred Space*. New York: Ballantine Books, 1995.

——. *Space Clearing*. Chicago, IL: Contemporary Books, 2000.

Marcus, Clare Cooper. *House as a Mirror of Self*. Berkeley, CA: Conari Press, 1995.

McDowell, Christopher Forrest and Tricia Clark-McDowell. *The Sanctuary Garden*. New York: Fireside, 1998.

Renard, John. *The Handy Religion Answer Book*. Canton, MI: Visible Ink Press, 2002.

Silbey, Uma. *Enlightenment on the Run*. San Rafael, CA: Airo Press, 1994.

Smith, Huston. *The Illustrated World's Religions*. San Francisco, CA: Harper San Francisco, 1994.

Storm, Hyemeyohsts. *Seven Arrows*. New York: Ballantine Books, 1973.

Streep, Peg. *Altars Made Easy*. San Francisco, CA: Harper San Francisco, 1997.

——. *Spiritual Gardening*. Alexandria, VA: Time-Life Books, 1999.

Sullivan, Kevin. *The Crystal Handbook*. New York: Signet, 1987.

Walker, Barbara G. *The Women's Dictionary of Symbols and Sacred Objects*. San Francisco, CA: Harper San Francisco, 1988.

Walsh, Roger, M.D., Ph.D. *Essential Spirituality*. New York: John Wiley and Sons, 1999.

Wydra, Nancilee. *Feng Shui in the Garden*. Chicago, IL: Contemporary Books, 1997.

Index

About the Author

 hawne Mitchell is a leading feng shui consultant, Realtor, writer, speaker, and workshop leader based in Santa Barbara, California. Over the past 20 years, through her consulting practice, she has helped hundreds of clients find and create life-affirming home and office environments. She may be contacted via her Website: *www.soulstyle.com*.

Shawne is also the author of *Exploring Feng Shui: Ancient Secrets and Modern Insight for Love, Joy and Abundance* (New Page Books, 2002). Shawne is the former Home Sanctuary Editor for *Healing Retreats and Spas* magazine, for which she contributed regular features articles and the column "Ask Shawne." Her writing has also appeared in magazines such as *Whole Life Times*, *Feng Shui Journal*, *Magical Blend*, *Casa Classic Homes*, and the *Santa Barbara News Press*, and in the spiritual anthology *More Hot Chocolate for the Mystical Soul*.

A graduate of the University of Washington, Shawne is a candidate for a master's degree in Spiritual Psychology. She received her feng shui training in the classic tradition of the Black Hat Sect of Tantric Buddhism. She has been a practitioner of Transcendental Meditation for 25 years.

Feng Shui Services, Books, Lectures, and Workshops

*S*hawne Mitchell is available to lecture, teach workshops, and provide feng shui consultations for homes, spas and resorts, Realtors, and businesses both nationally and internationally. For more information contact:

> Shawne Mitchell
> Soul Style
> P.O. Box 5765
> Santa Barbara, CA. 93150
> Telephone: (805) 565-4014
> Website: *www.soulstyle.com*

Her previous book, *Exploring Feng Shui: Ancient Secrets and Modern Insight for Love, Joy and Abundance* is available at most bookstores, or directly through Career Press Inc./ New Page Books at 1-800-227-3371.

Send Your Feng Shui Success Stories! It is often when hearing the success stories of others that we are motivated to change our own lives. Write to Shawne Mitchell with your personal success story at the previous address, or send it via e-mail through her Website. If you are willing to share your story with others, please include your written permission for her to publish it.